The Creative Squeeze

The Creative Squeeze

Getting the Most Out of Your Creative Team

Justin Price

Copyright © 2024 Justin Price

All rights reserved. No part of this publication may be reproduced, distributed, or transmitted in any form or by any means, including photocopying, recording, or other electronic or mechanical methods, without the prior written permission of the publisher, except in the case of brief quotations embodied in critical reviews and certain other non-commercial uses permitted by copyright law.

https://www.verscreative.com/book

Table of Contents

INTRODUCTION 13

01
~~Your team needs you to be the creative expert.~~ They need you to be the best visionary leader possible. 19

02
~~The path to success is the one that avoids failure.~~ Failure is necessary to achieve growth. 35

03
~~To get the most out of your team, push them as hard as you can.~~ Getting the most requires trust, respect, and balance. 49

04
~~Effective leaders push the organization from the top down.~~ You get the most out of your team by listening. 61

05
~~Standard Operating Procedures (SOPs) ruin great creative work.~~ SOPs make great work more consistent. 79

06
~~Growth means you should always be doing more.~~ Growth comes from doing the right things, not more things.   97

07
~~Guiding principles are corporate B.S.~~ Guiding principles are the backbone of your organization.   115

08
~~You can't measure creativity.~~ You can always measure the objective side of creative work.   133

ONE MORE THING   147

ABOUT THE AUTHOR   159

ACKNOWLEDGMENTS

I want to acknowledge all the people I've worked with over the past two decades who helped me navigate through the lies I once believed were sound leadership principles. Without those who were willing to tell me when I was wrong, point out a better path, and call out problems while helping me solve them, I wouldn't have developed the truths I hold today.

The most influential person in setting me on this path was John Campbell, the Senior Pastor at a church in Toledo where I worked at 19. To say he put up with a lot of my stupid mistakes would be an understatement. He loved me through many missteps, challenged me, and pushed me to figure things out. The work itself was important, but what stands out most from my time there is the students I mentored—people I met thanks to John's trust in me. Some of those students have gone on to achieve things far greater than anything I've done, and that continues to inspire me.

I think it's important for leaders to identify young people with hidden potential and provide them with opportunities to grow, even if that means giving them space to fail and learn from it. That's exactly what John did for me, and his mentorship set the tone for my career. I hope I'm just getting started. I'm excited about what the future looks like, and I want to acknowledge all of the people who will help me learn and grow throughout the remainder of my career.

The Creative Squeeze

INTRODUCTION

For those leading creative teams within an organization, a common question comes up in one way or another: How do I squeeze the most out of my creative team? Unfortunately, all the traditional notions of leadership, often portrayed as the "proper," "best," or even "award-winning," may not hold the key to unlocking the full potential of our teams.

I've been leading creative teams for over twenty years, and I have spent countless hours immersing myself in studies, books, seminars, and conferences, trying to emulate other's ideas into my own leadership style. But over the course of this time, I stumbled, failed, and struggled to fit into the boxes that other leaders laid out. I recognized my inner drive to push boundaries in order to discover the type of leader I needed to be for my creative teams. After two decades of digging, I unearthed a profound truth: the core of successful and brilliant work lies in serving the creatives first. I found that to get the most out of every creative team member, I must put them first. Considering what a creative needs will always produce a better outcome. The alternative is pushing them, asking for more, without even considering what they need from you.

My journey toward this realization was arduous, unconventional, and transformative.

THE CORE OF SUCCESSFUL AND BRILLIANT WORK LIES IN SERVING THE CREATIVES FIRST

Here's how I got there

I fell in love and married my high school sweetheart, Megan, someone with a chronic and complicated case of Lyme disease and a few lesser-known co-infections. In our early years of marriage, the symptoms were mild. There were more doctor's appointments than the average marriage, but that didn't stop us from traveling the country or building our careers - me as a creative director serving in the church and her as a pediatric nurse. But eventually, her health took a turn for the worse. Her team of doctors recommended that she stop working, forcing her to step down from a career she loved. My job supported us and allowed me to flex my hours as much as possible, but I was still working over 60 hours every week. As my caregiving responsibilities increased, it became more and more difficult to maintain my job and care for my wife.

With the loss of her salary and increased stress from medical bills piling up, I needed an outlet that would both raise our income and be flexible enough to meet our unique caregiving situation. I really didn't know what to do next, so I dove headfirst into freelancing with the creative skills I had developed.

As soon as I had made the decision to open myself up full-time, there was more work than I could handle alone. I hired two people - a part-time copywriter and a very green employee just one year out of college. The work grew in scope, which was exciting, but I found myself wearing multiple hats - the business owner, salesperson, creative team manager, web developer, graphic designer, brand manager, art director, executive producer, camera operator, equipment financier, editor, and creative director.

Everything shifted. I was no longer just focused on being a creative director, helping one organization at a time. I had a particular skill set that made me successful as a creative, but now my responsibilities had multiplied, and so had the demands on my time. I had to figure out how to juggle everything while ensuring the health and effectiveness of the small team I now led. I made an uneducated move based on financial considerations and the illusion of a better life. Almost instantly, this realization shed light on a lot of painful leadership lessons.

Simply put, I didn't know what I didn't know. I was completely unaware of the challenges ahead. Running a team that consistently delivered value to clients at every moment was a far tougher feat than I ever imagined. I had the creative talent to do most of what my clients were asking for on my own, but as my business, Vers Creative, grew, the gaps in my leadership training became glaringly evident. Managing and effectively leading creatives across diverse accounts required a level of skill that I was not equipped to handle.

Looking back on the first decade of my career before I started Vers, I believed a lot of traditional leadership principles applied to leading creatives. These were ideas I had read about or seen in the stories of other successful creatives. I held onto misguided advice from well-intentioned mentors and even recommendations from leaders that I later realized were driven by self-interest or fear. Now, I want to take those lies and offer a different perspective - one that I developed through leading creatives while experiencing the struggles of my own life circumstances.

As I write this, Vers Creative is turning 10 years old and is one of the best agencies in the country serving nonprofits and faith-based organizations. I'm proud of where we are now and looking forward to what is ahead, but the road to get here wasn't necessarily a road.

Introduction

Sometimes, it felt more like the rocky cliffside mule trail that guides people down into the basin of a canyon.

In this book, I unpack the most essential lessons I've learned leading creatives, exposing lies I heard along the way, and defining new truths. The chapters will challenge your preconceptions, expand your perspective, and guide you toward leading in a way that helps you squeeze the most out of your team.

CHAPTER

Lie: Your team needs you to be the creative **expert**.

Truth: They need you to be the **best visionary leader** possible.

01

The Creative Squeeze

When I was a senior in high school, I dove headfirst into my first real leadership experience as a church worship leader. As time went on, my responsibilities grew from leading a band to running tech and then from planning the services to handling all of the church communications. By the time I was in my mid 20's, I had a great start to my career with two quickly growing organizations as proof of my success. I found myself accepting the position of Creative Director at a mega-church — a huge opportunity for a 25-year-old. But leading multiple teams at such a young age came with a series of humbling events that showed me I wasn't the best at everything. There were people more skilled and talented than I was at pretty much everything I was supposed to oversee. It was a hard pill to swallow that took a long time to fully come to grips with.

I assumed that since I had been promoted, I had all the answers and that my team could only learn from me. I thought I was naturally the best and entered into the position full of pride. It took a friend named Matt Sanders to help me realize just how much lower my talent was from those around me. Matt is a remarkable musician whose talent exceeded my own. Recognizing his gift and potential, I invited him, well I convinced him, to join the team, knowing in my gut that his expertise would only make us better. Bringing Matt on board wasn't just about adding talent; it was a lesson in humility for me. Taking that step from leading on stage to now being in the back of the room unlocked a new perspective for me as a leader.

It allowed me to gain insights I couldn't see from the front. Creative Directors don't usually get that vantage point, but this new role forced me to get out of the way. I realized that holding onto the spotlight would be detrimental to the success of the team, preventing other people from realizing their own gifts.

This new perspective solidified the principle that leadership isn't about being the know-it-all, having it all together, and being the best; it's about empowering those who know more than me to do what they were created to do. While I was challenged to grow as a leader, I had to let go of the creative work I loved. That's one of the most ironic things about leading a creative team. The more successful your team becomes, the less involved you ultimately are with the hands-on, creative work. I had to learn that it wasn't about me and the skills I mastered. It was about setting a clear direction and vision for where we were going and letting my team solve the problems within the nuances of their expertise. When I was finally able to grasp this concept, my career skyrocketed. It became clear that I didn't have to know everything. My job was now about allowing the real experts to shine by being the visionary they needed.

Over the past few years, I've had my fair share of moments where I hoped my team would just magically find the solutions to specific challenges. I'd throw tasks their way without much explanation or direction. That approach never panned out well, and it wasn't because my team lacked the skills. It was because I wasn't leading with a clear vision. Once that realization hit me, everything changed. I realized the importance of clearly communicating my vision and giving my team the chance to truly get on board. Getting their buy-in with any project is absolutely essential for success.

Each team member is going to evolve at their own pace and develop different skills. But by reorienting your approach to create an environment that prioritizes collaboration and mutual support, you pave the way for a healthy team dynamic that is continuously growing. To do this, three primary mindset shifts need to take place.

Mindset Shift 1
Transition from passion for the work to passion for leadership.

This is the first and hardest shift to make. To put it simply, being an impactful leader requires taking the time to identify what truly motivates you and, in turn, deciding on what parts of your work you're willing to release. As a creative, you love to make things, and you've developed a variety of particular skills throughout your life that have made you the person you are today. Embracing the experience of your creative journey involves understanding that your passions are not just random hobbies, they are integral to your unique leadership style and voice.

Being an artist clicked for me during that awkward middle school age when everyone is just trying to fit in and understand themselves. Drawing was my first love, but it wasn't until my eighth-grade teacher introduced me to painting that I truly felt the power of artistic expression. At the same time, I stumbled upon a community of fellow music enthusiasts who shared my passion. Music and painting worked together to create a connection with other people in a way that I had struggled with before. I felt a sense of belonging and purpose.

I tell you this to highlight that creatives often find themselves building a career out of some of the deepest parts of their identity. After all, as much as parents want their kids to develop artistic skills, you never hear them expressing hope that their child ends up being a starving artist. Whether you make music, visuals, or any other form of creative expression, you got to where you are today because something deep inside drove you to cultivate skills. Oftentimes this motivation is rooted in experiences that are deeply personal, with creative work existing as a way to process the pain you might have felt during difficult seasons in your life. There are endless stories of how creative work functions as an outlet that provides hope and connection to others, giving people a purpose when life's challenges make it feel like there are none.

The deeply personal nature of creative work is exactly why it is so difficult to give up in order to prioritize the work of your team. This doesn't mean fully stopping the creative acts that bring you joy, but rather changing your perspective about the skills you've developed along the way in order to better lead others. Sometimes it can feel like you're actually sacrificing the most fun parts of your job. But in exchanging them for leadership responsibilities, you actually end up bringing an even greater value to your organization. Plus, the skills you've developed are still there. I still draw and paint as a way to relax or pick up my guitar at home to play for my wife and daughter. Our staff at Vers is always ready for me to jump on the drums for a 10-minute jam session between meetings. But this is no longer the primary value that I am bringing to work everyday.

YOU HAVE TO BE WILLING TO LET GO OF YOUR ART AND EMBRACE A LEADERSHIP MINDSET

The deep love for your skill can be a hurdle to overcome. Mastering your craft is rewarding, and not everyone feels called to let that go. Sometimes, the desire for individual success overshadows the need to elevate others. A leader would rather be in the spotlight than raise up the people around them. Yet, this mindset doesn't foster an environment for fellow creatives to thrive. Please hear me loud and clear - there is nothing wrong with this mindset. It's okay if you want to hold tight to the work you love; it just won't help you create an environment where other creatives can live up to their potential. For some, the whole goal of getting really good at something is to lead, as opposed to raising up other leaders. It's a crossroads where you must decide: Do I continue as an individual contributor or evolve into a great leader? Throughout my career, I have consistently wrestled with this idea, and so should you. In order to become a great leader, you have to be willing to let go of your art and embrace a leadership mindset to cultivate a high-performing team. In doing so, you end up becoming the curator, not the creator.

Gut Check

Take time to reflect on your career and how you came into this leadership position.

Write down your story.

Now, think about yourself as a leader today.

Have you fully embraced your role?

Do you think you need to be the expert?

If you do, what is preventing you from letting go of that mindset?

Think about what you will gain from raising up those you lead.

Mindset Shift 2
Think like a long-term investor.

When I'm talking to other leaders, I often hear, "It takes more time for someone else to do the work than to just do it myself. Why would I pay for someone else to do it?"

When I hear this, my first instinct is to assume that systems, processes, communication, and reporting remain underdeveloped. While this is almost never as exciting as diving into creative work, it's crucial to creating the healthiest work environment possible. You will need to construct your organization's foundation from the ground up, and much like any building project, there is a cost.

An easy objection is that designated funds are not currently in the budget. As easy as this response is, it's usually the case that the person responsible for scrutinizing these expenditures is looking at this as a cost, not an investment. They're doing their job and protecting the numbers in front of them. That's a natural tendency for the human brain - to protect what's already there. It's a more difficult process to stretch our minds to be willing to take calculated risks for greater gains. But the bottom line is that investing in a healthy culture demands not just this change in mindset but also a journey in skill development.

If you're leading within a non-profit and believe that profitable business principles don't apply, you're lying to yourself. Regardless of funding sources—be it grants, donations, or an internal revenue stream—nobody wants to support an inefficient organization. It's baffling to witness decisions where spending is slashed, and investments in people and organizational growth are denied in the name of "saving money." Solely focusing on saving money is a shortsighted approach that can rapidly sink your ship.

Building a healthy culture isn't just a feel-good initiative—it's a smart financial move. It cuts down costs associated with hiring and firing, which often end up as unplanned expenses. From my experience, hiring a new employee with a salary ranging from $50,000 to $100,000 can incur an additional cost of $25,000. This includes the hours spent by human resources, travel expenses for out-of-town candidates, trial periods, and the lengthy process of training and onboarding. Skipping the careful hiring process and ending up with the wrong person could add another $25,000 to your expenses. Moreover, firing is emotionally taxing for the whole team and may involve severance payments or attempts at improvement, each with its own additional costs.

Now, if you are walking into this journey thinking money is not an issue, that's great. But what about time? It's crucial to recognize the intricate relationship between money and time. Money is cyclical, but time is a limited resource. The constraints of both often go hand in hand, impacting our ability to navigate the challenges our organizations face.

Time is frequently under-budgeted, undervalued, and overlooked. If I'm being honest, budgeting time can be the Achilles' heel of many creative teams. The misconception that there is never enough time to achieve optimal results pervades many creative processes. The reality is that creative productions, no matter how intricate, can always be refined and enhanced, leading to a continuous cycle of work.

But it's not just about logging hours to complete a project. I believe the greatest thing you can do for your team is invest YOUR TIME into building a healthy culture. If you are willing to invest the time, you will gain that back in productivity. Think about it this way - studies conducted by the University of Oxford and the University of Warwick concluded that people who are happy are 13% more productive in their jobs. It's up to you to create the space for your team to thrive - and that's a skill. It's a conscious choice to prioritize your people as the highest return on investment.

Teams I work with often appeal to a similar baseline fear that even after taking the time to invest in their development, team members might leave. I could give you ten pages of stories, exposing the scars I carry about this, but for now, just trust me. The concern about losing a well-trained team member should not deter you from investing more in your people. Investing time into creating a healthy culture will not only attract great talent but also allow you to retain your highest performers, paying back dividends over time. This perspective shift sets the stage for a dynamic workplace where everyone thrives.

> **THE GREATEST THING YOU CAN DO FOR YOUR TEAM IS INVEST YOUR TIME INTO BUILDING A HEALTHY CULTURE**

I genuinely believe that I work harder because the individuals on my team possess incredible talent, and I'm constantly striving to match their level of excellence. There is a cyclical nature to it. By creating and sustaining an environment that enables my team to perform at their peak, I am continually inspired to refine my own approach and rise to the occasion.

Mindset Shift 3
Adopt technology as a necessary creative tool.

Before you roll your eyes at this title, hear me out. This section might as well be just for me, to remind myself of the importance of embracing new things. The longer I'm in leadership the harder it is to push myself to seek out fresh perspectives and adopt innovative new approaches. I think we all would be more comfortable if we could just use the same tools from when we first started — the same software, the same computers, the same workflow.

But the world is changing rapidly, and sticking to the old ways can render you and your team obsolete. At this point in history, there is very little that comes anywhere near the value of adopting new technologies. In order to stay relevant and effective, there are few things you can do that are more important than fostering a culture of continuous adaptability.

In college, I devoted myself to studying oil painting for three years. I built my entire schedule around it, carving out time to research and find inspiration, and reserving every Friday for painting. I looked forward to it all week, spending time in museums and retail spaces, taking architecture tours, and blocking out all other distractions so I could spend time creating. Looking back now, it's crazy how inefficient and slow it all seems in comparison to the amount of research I can do and work I can produce digitally without ever leaving my office. That change from being a studio artist who paints to a digital creator was challenging but it has paid off by being able to create art faster and more scalable in order to bring value to paying clients.

This mindset shift is particularly important for those who worked in the tech space before 2021. This next wave of technology will impact humanity in a way that is both exciting and also terrifying. It's no longer an option to ignore cutting-edge tech as leaders. It's essential to remain aware and keep integration as a main priority. It doesn't have to be your role to lead technological change, but it's also important to not be a roadblock either. I see so many teams struggle with this, navigating leaders who are standing in the way of an organization that wants to move forward. Resistance will only slow you down, causing you to miss out on helpful tech, or risk losing a team who moves on without you. What's at risk is an organization that is on its way to being outdated, irrelevant, or even worse…extinct.

Take artificial intelligence. The AI revolution has transformed technology into a strategic partner, creating space for teams to focus on what truly matters. By automating routine tasks, AI enhances efficiency, freeing up time for a deeper dive into innovation. It acts as a collaborator, analyzing data to reveal patterns that spark fresh ideas and elevate the creative process. AI goes even further to provide personalized recommendations, tailoring its support to individual team members' preferences and strengths. This shift in mindset goes beyond viewing technology as a mere tool; it recognizes it as a game-changing ally that propels creative teams toward excellence.

What it All Means

True leadership isn't about holding onto the spotlight or being the expert in every aspect of the creative process. It's about empowering others to shine and fostering an environment where everyone's talents are valued. Transitioning from being the focal point of creativity to becoming a curator of talent has been both challenging and rewarding for me. It's a journey that has taught me the value of mindset shifts, from prioritizing leadership over individual success to investing in the long-term growth of my team and embracing technology as a strategic partner. By applying these shifts, I've not only seen my team thrive but also found inspiration to continually refine my own approach. I challenge you to really analyze your leadership style. Look ahead and focus on a journey of growth for yourself and your team, empowering them so you can collectively achieve greatness beyond what you could accomplish alone.

_____
_____
_____

Action Steps

01
DO the gut check after Mindset Shift 1.

02
Set aside time and resources for leadership training and mentorship for yourself and your team members in order to create a culture of learning and growth.

03
Allocate resources for developing efficient systems and processes. Advocate for investments in organizational growth, even in non-profit settings.

04
Dedicate time to refining processes post-meetings, and conducting regular reviews to identify areas for improvement in systems.

05
Continue reading on to develop strategies to build and maintain a healthy workplace culture that attracts and retains top talent.

CHAPTER

Chapter 02

Lie: The path to success is the one that avoids failure.

Truth: Failure is necessary to achieve growth.

We often struggle to distinguish between healthy and unhealthy forms of failure. Healthy failure is characterized by learning, resilience, constructive feedback, innovation, and accountability, while unhealthy failure involves blame, repetitive patterns, fear, negative self-talk, and lack of support. It's important to recognize that failing can be the quickest (and sometimes most painful) path to both personal and team growth.

If your team is afraid of failure, they'll never get anywhere. Even if they have the potential to push past boundaries, it's your responsibility as a leader to set the expectation that it's essential to take risks that might result in failure. The best leaders encourage their teams to move beyond their comfort zones, pushing them to the point of encountering failures. Remember, the overall growth achieved through embracing failure is far greater than the growth achieved without it.

GUT CHECK

What is your relationship with failure?

Do you avoid it at all costs?

As a leader, do you truly embrace failure as an opportunity to learn and grow?

Are you building a culture where your team feels safe to fail?

Chapter 02

The Unique Relationships With Failure

A transformative journey happens when we can understand the value of learning from our mistakes, both personally and professionally. A core part of our DNA at Vers is trying to find fail points. That's how we grow but also how we push our clients to grow. I am genuinely thrilled when a leader expresses a desire for their organization to achieve exponential growth. One of our agency's standout skills is our expertise in reverse-engineering desired growth by constructing a conservative plan in a step-by-step strategy. For leaders with a growth-centric mindset, this strategy might as well be a treasure map, charting the course to where they want to ultimately take their organization.

Over the years, I've noticed that it's often not a lack of resources or a strong team that holds creative teams back. Instead, the primary roadblock to exponential growth is fear, and three distinct approaches typically unfold once a leader is presented with this turnkey plan:

1. Fear of Failure

When some leaders see a roadmap for growth, they encounter a roadblock of fear. They hesitate and, in some cases, choose not to take any steps forward. This hesitation is rooted in any number of doubts, from concerns about their team to personal convictions, an inconsistent income model, or the actual work the roadmap proposes. Unfortunately, when an organization is frozen with fear, it can lead to missed opportunities and even backward steps.

At Vers, we've seen leaders come to us for solutions but end up choosing to stick to familiar routines, believing that playing it safe is the better path. However, it's crucial for leaders to recognize that doing nothing can significantly impact revenue and market positioning. The bottom line is, don't be like them. We've done the work and laid it all out, demonstrating the potential your organization has to make a lasting impact. But sometimes, we never get to watch it happen. This is definitely the hardest part of our job because we see leaders with a deep desire for massive growth never achieve it because they're paralyzed by fear.

2. Misunderstanding Failure's Role

Some leaders fail to recognize the pivotal role that failure plays in their journey. They struggle to assess risks effectively and neglect to allocate time for the necessary small failures that pave the way for success. Instead, they tend to dive headfirst into initiatives, frequently taking on more than they can handle. This approach results in a significant expenditure of time and money, but the return on investment (ROI) remains elusive. As a consequence, projects, initiatives, advertising expenditures, and staffing efforts are prematurely halted, and the entire investment ends up going to waste.

I can personally empathize with this challenge from my early days as an agency owner. There were instances where I initiated marketing campaigns, and my team invested considerable effort in creating advertisements, emails, landing pages, and offers to launch them quickly. However, I sometimes failed to account for the time needed to fine-tune and optimize these campaigns for tangible and sustained results. Regrettably, I canceled these initiatives prematurely, which worked to demotivate my team, and caused them to hesitate on new marketing strategies in the future out of fear that I might halt their progress again.

3. Embracing Failure

The third and most successful relationship with failure requires acknowledging its presence. This approach encourages leaders to take an iterative path toward growth, allowing for small failures along the way.

When we begin campaign development, we take a highly conservative approach. This means we make the smallest possible moves and test them thoroughly to see what works and what doesn't. Our goal is to fail as fast as possible so we can quickly change course and focus on more productive paths forward. This proactive mindset not only accelerates the learning curve but also allows us to leverage failures as stepping stones toward success.

At Vers, this approach has contributed to an impressive 87% annual client retention rate, an achievement made possible by setting realistic expectations and addressing issues methodically. There is no BS. No fluff. I've seen too many instances where marketers think optimistically when selling to a potential client. They over-promise and under-deliver. But with any creative process, you have to look at what outcome is best vs. what's the most realistic. It's important to have an understanding of both. We have to ask ourselves: What is possible? What is the most probable outcome? What is this going to cost? What is possible with our budget and resources? These questions are often skipped but the truth is that answering these can still be a really exciting conversation to have.

I have found that being honest with myself, my team and the clients we serve has allowed for trust to be built and longtime relationships to be repeated. That's how we have maintained our retention rate. The reality is that we do better work when we take the most realistic approach and only put time and energy into something that we know will deliver results.

You Are Not Your Work.

It's crucial to extend the same approach we offer our clients to our own teams. A team that can embrace failure becomes more resilient and adaptable. They learn to pivot quickly, experiment with new approaches, and innovate without hesitation. I've worked hard to establish an environment at Vers where mistakes are viewed as opportunities for growth rather than reasons for blame. There is the understanding that setbacks are a natural part of any project and can provide valuable insights into why something happened and how we can do better next time. I want my team to feel safe to take risks, share their ideas openly, and learn from both their successes and failures. If everyone consistently hits their goals, then we didn't set the bar high enough.

At Vers, we've been intentional about building a team of self-motivators who look for opportunities to push boundaries. It's bravery that gets celebrated internally as a way to encourage everyone to be bold enough to take chances. No matter the meeting or setting, we intentionally take those opportunities to call out a team member for their work, even if it didn't have the result we planned. As the leader, building failure into your culture means your team aims to set goals that will prevent them from failing. They should be trying to do things they have never done before.

A TEAM THAT EMBRACES FAILURE BECOMES MORE RESILIENT AND ADAPTABLE

Many people shy away from taking risks because they lack trust or their identity is too tied to their work. As leaders, it's crucial that we separate ourselves from the work when we give feedback. Remember, feedback is about the work, not a critique of the person. It's my responsibility to guide my team through their failures and help them learn from those experiences. If a team member fails, it's on me to communicate that constructively and supportively. Taking ownership of these failures as a leader builds trust and fosters a stronger, more resilient team.

For example, one of the most challenging creative projects is a website. Web development became an essential skill around the same time I started my creative career, and its evolution has always run parallel to my life as a creative leader. If I'm being honest, the creative process behind web development has kicked my butt more than any other project or service that we provide. Websites are an essential business asset, so they attract the eyes of more decision-makers who all need to give their opinions and approval, and all think they know more than the experts. Over time, this has the potential to get expensive particularly for a thing that is always changing and getting updated. Plus, if there is one thing I've learned, it's that our eyes are always bigger than our wallets, so the vision of what the decision-makers want isn't always realistic for their budgets.

Web projects are challenging because they involve so many different forms of media. To be successful, they need great copy with images and videos that connect with the copy to tell a story. That's not even mentioning the code itself, the hosting, and how things are set up to create a natural, easy-to-use experience for the audience. Plus, there's the marketing. Setting up tracking and analytics in order to understand how people are using the website and using what you've learned to generate leads.

Because all of these factors are important, we've had to build multiple checkpoints to test for failure. During the first five years of selling websites, I often found that the team thought the website was done when they finished their specific tasks. But the reality is that once all of those aspects are done, we're really only halfway through the process. Gaining experience in website development was the perfect way for me to realize something that is true for every creative project: even the best will fail at delivering a complete experience. What becomes important is setting expectations and building time into budgets to rework things in order to get the best version and results possible.

For creatives, there is a constant tension between knowing what we're capable of and coming to grips with things that don't meet our expectations. Most of us are programmed to see our potential but aren't as skilled at wrestling with the truth that great work takes time and failure. It's impossible to make anything great if you're only thinking about the obstacles standing in your way. It's about striking the right balance between all of the mitigating risks and factoring in extra time into the budget in order to produce the best work possible.

But, keep in mind that not all team members may easily embrace the idea of failure. Many creatives struggle to separate their self-worth from their work. They resist accepting feedback or the notion that their work could encounter setbacks, believing that they must achieve perfection in order to succeed. It's imperative to convey the message that this mindset shift is essential.

As a leader, if you've successfully navigated the mindset shifts outlined in Chapter 1, you've likely recognized the need to take a step back from your own individual work and embrace the role of leadership. Now, your responsibility is to assist your team in distancing themselves from the belief that perfection is the only path to success and growth.

Reflecting on my journey, I have learned firsthand that living out this concept is far more challenging than describing it. If I could go back and talk with a younger version of myself, I would emphasize that the work does not define me. It's ok to fail. Despite the discomfort it brings in the moment, failure has a way of unfolding into valuable learning experiences.

What it All Means

Failure is a natural part of the creative process. As leaders, we have to look at mistakes and setbacks not as roadblocks but as stepping stones toward improvement. It's about fostering a work environment where our teams feel empowered to take risks and explore new ideas without fear bearing down on them. When we create this kind of atmosphere where innovation is encouraged, and boundaries are meant to be pushed, we unlock the true potential of our team. Trust me, when your crew knows they have the freedom to experiment and the safety of a leader to support them, that's when the real magic happens.

_____
_____
_____

Action Steps

01
Revise team goals to incorporate experiments that carry the potential for failure.

02
Encourage your team to view failures as opportunities for innovation and course correction.

03
Publicly acknowledge and celebrate healthy failures during team meetings and one-on-one discussions.

04
Address and question any existing biases or fears surrounding failure within the organizational culture during major planning or team meetings.

05
Ensure that all recurring processes include a step for improvement when failures are identified.

Chapter 02

CHAPTER

Lie: To get the most out of your team, push them as hard as you can.

Truth: Getting the most requires trust, respect, and balance.

03

The Creative Squeeze

As a creative director in the 21st century, it's hard not to be inspired by figures like Steve Jobs and Elon Musk. Both stand out as prolific, creative thinkers with long track records of disrupting industries and pushing the boundaries of what's possible. I have used Apple products for as long as I can remember and always made time to watch Jobs introduce new products, explaining the creativity behind their development and revolutionary impact on everyday life. I've also learned a lot watching Musk's career, and the way he has transcended industries and made an impact on everything from sustainable energy to space exploration.

What has fascinated me about both men is their ability to isolate their own visions and not be influenced by outside noise. I often return to a famous quote from Jobs where he says: "Some people say, 'Give the customers what they want.' But that's not my approach. Our job is to figure out what they're going to want before they do." Both Jobs and Musk built careers on their ability to read things that aren't yet on the page. They anticipate future needs and create demand for innovative solutions before the market even realizes a gap exists.

While many have tried to emulate Jobs and Musk, applying their philosophies and actions to our own circumstances can be challenging. This has to do, in part, with what we know about both of their personal lives. A common theme in stories about Jobs was that much of his life was spent not listening to anyone but himself, relying on his own internal drive to push ideas and projects forward. So, if this approach contributed to his success, why would we not want to replicate his way of thinking? Here's the thing: we can't look at his professional triumphs without acknowledging his personal sacrifices – the brokenness, turmoil, and resentment that came with it, especially from those closest to him. While Jobs left a significant impact on the tech world, there's no guide titled "How to Build a Great Culture and Community" by Steve Jobs.

While there are countless things to draw inspiration from within the life of Steve Jobs, we should also be cautious about whether we want to follow in his footsteps entirely. His methodology worked for him, but it came with a steep mental, physical, and relational cost. Every biography of Jobs is filled with stories of staff burnout, strained relationships, and unreasonable behavior with no remorse. While these traits are often deemed necessary for achieving monumental breakthroughs, for most, the success isn't worth the pain of this type of leadership.

Musk shares a similar story about his climb to the top. Behind many of his achievements, there are reports of intense work environments at Tesla and SpaceX and Musk's own admission of sleeping on the factory floor to show his employees that he was 100% committed to being there. While there is a sense in which this level of commitment inspires me, other details in Musk's life highlight a significant imbalance. He has told stories of committing himself so fully to a task that he has had to go to a friend's house in Hawaii or get lost in a video game for days just to recover in order to meet the level of intensity with the opposite extreme. Musk's unyielding drive and resilience have propelled his companies to unprecedented heights, but they also spotlight the potential personal and professional costs involved. As a leader, the example set at the top will trickle down, potentially normalizing a cycle of high stress and burnout as the standard for success.

The leadership style depicted in these biographies is marked by significant consequences: split families, bad relationships with kids, strained friendships, and business partnerships. Things that probably do not align with your goals and values. It's crucial to recognize that effective leadership doesn't have to be an all-or-nothing approach. Of course, it's natural to be ambitious, but we can't lose sight of what truly matters—the relationships we have with loved ones and our own health and well-being.

I've felt the regret of missed moments with my daughter and seen the consequences of sacrificing family time for work. But I've also experienced the joy that comes from choosing to be present for my family. My work is always better when I am intentional about spending time with my wife at night, catching up on what happened in the day, dreaming, reading, and praying together. It's a daily tension to manage, but the moments I succeed in prioritizing my family are more rewarding than any professional achievement.

It took me a while to realize that when my work-life balance tilts too heavily toward work, it not only affects my family but also impacts my team. If I am so caught up in work and start contacting my team at off-hours or pushing them to join additional meetings or even travel beyond what they signed up for, then I am setting the example of what I deem an acceptable lifestyle. I don't want that for them. I want them to see me prioritizing my wife and daughter so they feel empowered to do the same.

Rather than replicating Jobs' and Musk's philosophies, I want to advocate for a "new school" of thinking. The focus is on learning from their mistakes, applying universally effective leadership principles, avoiding imitation, and shaping organizational culture without imposing undue burdens. My goal is to present an alternative approach distinct from the observed practices of many organizations.

GUT CHECK

Are you a "Steve Jobs?" Does your leadership style reflect the "all or nothing" approach that sets unreasonable expectations and limits the feedback of your team?

Or are you more of an Elon Musk, struggling with a lack of balance and unhealthy boundaries?

Are you willing to accept that greatness can come from a "new school" approach to leadership?

"New School" Thought (Part 1): Start with empathy

Understanding our team's problems and navigating challenges that arise during projects are crucial aspects of effective leadership. But I have to be honest. Empathy and compassion are not natural strengths of mine. I was raised believing that through hard work, you could accomplish anything—and that failure was a result of not trying. My developmental years were filled with watching my dad work hard to build a business that would give my family a better life than what he had as a kid. I learned a lot watching him overcome obstacles and make sacrifices, but it didn't teach me to be empathetic for those who could not accomplish similar feats. Reflecting on my own experiences, I realize I had privileges others didn't, which made it difficult for me to understand their perspectives.

REALIZING EMPATHY'S PIVOTAL ROLE IN PROVIDING TEAM STABILITY FUNDAMENTALLY SHAPED HOW I APPROACH MY OWN TEAM

My late wife's illness provided me with a profound lesson in empathy. Caring for her while her disease slowly progressed required me to consider what was within her control and what wasn't every single day. This personal experience, unlike anything a book could teach, became a powerful source of growth as a leader. I began to think of empathy not as a reason to lower expectations but as a posture in which you address expectations.

Witnessing Megan deteriorate emphasized the value of stability. For me, this meant feeling safe and being allowed to make mistakes without severe consequences. This kind of stability is crucial for optimal creative work, as low stability introduces threats to accounts, jobs, and team cohesion. Realizing the pivotal role empathy plays in providing stability for a team fundamentally shaped how I approach my own team. As leaders, we have to recognize that while empathy may not come naturally to everyone, it can still be cultivated and nurtured through education and practice. Empathy exists on a spectrum, and individuals may vary in their capacity for empathy across different situations and relationships.

Over the course of my two decades of creative work, I've witnessed a number of situations impact performance. Whether it's the health of a loved one, moving to a new state, a spouse changing jobs, kid's schedules, or marriage problems, these challenges are unavoidable and should actually be embraced. If you're unwilling to navigate these realities, you might be in the wrong job. Embracing all of life's challenges with empathy allows us to cultivate a work environment filled with love, resilience, and unwavering support, where every member feels valued and empowered to thrive.

"New School" Thought (part 2): Figure out their fulfillment, excitement, & frustrations

Recently, I had a meeting with a newer team member, Collin. He was definitely dedicated and always willing to do whatever was needed, but the effort on a strategy I assigned wasn't seeing much results. After a few months of this, I sensed his frustration and opened a conversation about his day-to-day responsibilities.

Drawing from my empathy and listening skills while leaning into Collin's strengths, I proposed a change—focusing on video and audio editing for our podcast, "The Nonprofit Renaissance." One conversation led to a small shift that demonstrated care for Collin's frustration, allowing me to put him in a better position. (By the way, Collin is crushing the podcast.)

When listening to your team, try to focus on three categories of thoughts and feelings:

1. Fulfillment

- Maintain a long-term connection to each individual's values and life goals.
- Understand what brings meaning to their life and contributes to their overall mission and drive.

2. Excitement

- Discover what they are currently working on or involved in that excites them.
- Stoke the fire and share similar moments to enhance enthusiasm.

3. Frustration

- Your team's frustrations are often overlooked but valuable for improvement.
- Understand what is driving them crazy or what they wish to change so that you can pivot away from demotivating tasks.

At Vers, we call these "temperature checks." These check-ins gauge a person's overall fulfillment and identify areas where they can make impactful changes.

What it All Means

Remember, your organization's success is intertwined with the growth and fulfillment of your team members. By actively fostering empathy, encouraging individual growth, and adapting to evolving circumstances, you create a culture that not only retains high-performing creatives but also propels the organization forward.

_____
_____
_____

Action Steps

01
Listen with an empathetic ear to identify each team member's fulfilling and exciting work. Your role is to find or create ways for this work to constitute a significant part of their job expectations.

02
Recognize and accept that team members face various personal challenges that can impact their performance. Embrace these realities as part of the professional landscape, and strive to accommodate and support your team accordingly.

03
Continuously gauge your team's overall fulfillment, excitement, and frustrations. Actively seek feedback on what motivates and demotivates them.

04
Make impactful changes to address your team members' needs and concerns. This may involve adjusting their roles, tasks, or responsibilities to better align with their interests and strengths, ultimately fostering stability and enhancing team performance.

05
Acknowledge that cultivating empathy is a unique human ability that AI cannot replace. Hold onto this aspect closely, and recognize its value in creating a healthy culture within the team. Utilize the extra time gained from creative squeeze opportunities to invest in empathetic leadership.

CHAPTER

Chapter 04

Lie: Effective leaders push the organization from the top down.

Truth: You get the most out of your team by listening.

04

Any leadership training worth it's salt will typically feature some sort of engagement with active listening. But as common as these conversations are, active listening really is more than a buzzword. It's the key to building the strongest foundation for your team. Active listening involves ensuring that you not only hear what someone is saying but that you can effectively articulate feedback that confirms your understanding. This kind of communication fosters trust and transparency among team members, allowing them to feel valued, heard, and works to enhance overall collaboration that drives better results.

Like you, I had heard about active listening for decades and did my best to practice it, but admittedly was not always successful. For me, it was the prime example of "knowing does not always equal doing." As I think back on my career in leadership, there are plenty of conversations I can think of with staff that haunt me to this day, where I wonder what went wrong in our communication. Times when my team didn't seem to understand the vision I was trying to share, resulting in a sense of frustration from them and from me. In any conversation, the two cardinal sins are wasting time and communicating in a way that leads to frustration. Active listening is the best way that I have found to avoid both.

Feedback is an essential part of creative work, and as a leader, I used to find myself going into "fix it mode" right off the bat. I love to be helpful and know that whether it's a logo design, a video edit, or a marketing strategy, my insight could be useful in making things better. After years of operating this way, I found that my vision was having a negative impact. If I inserted my "fix" without an active conversation, it would devalue what they had done and demotivate them to do better work on their own. This resulted in me losing the trust of the team, which is about the worst feeling possible as a leader.

I realized that I was dealing with two competing problems. The first was that I was too eager to jump to my own opinion and lacked the humility to actively listen to what my team was trying to communicate to me. The second was insecurity. I so badly wanted to prove my value and position myself as an expert that I put my own pride over my team. I subconsciously thought that since I had the most experience, my ideas would naturally be the best. It makes me a little sick to my stomach today thinking about all the great creatives I've worked with who had incredible ideas that they never got to try because my pride stopped me from listening to them.

There was one specific meeting in 2015 where a team member called me out on some critical feedback they had received and made a case for why they thought their work had been good. In doing so, they helped me understand where they were coming from and gave me an ultimate "Aha!" moment. I realized that my job as a leader was not to push them further with a critical eye and point out what I thought were shortcomings. Instead, it was my job to lead them with an inquisitive mind, asking questions to better understand their process and expectations. I realized that in order to be the best leader I could be, I needed to listen well—ask deeper questions, and unpack the hang-ups that were creating a gap between my expectations and the work I was evaluating.

Creative work is personal, and managing a creative team presents unique challenges that demand active listening and heightened emotional intelligence. This involves recognizing, processing, and managing not only your emotions but also those of your team members. While mind-reading skills may not be our forte, effective leaders can come close to knowing what their team is thinking by building a culture of open communication. It's about asking the right questions in the right setting, ensuring you listen and comprehend the answers in order to consistently understand what motivates, frustrates, and excites your creative team.

> **I REALIZED THAT IN ORDER TO BE THE BEST LEADER I COULD BE, I NEEDED TO LISTEN WELL**

It's important to avoid focusing on weaknesses. Think about your school days when one "F" overshadowed a report card full of "A's." Creatives don't respond well to a fixation on their "F's." In fact, most of them invest a considerable amount of time and energy into hiding these shortcomings. It's not always as simple as learning new skills. Every second that a creative spends on improving their weaknesses is time taken away from excelling in areas where they naturally shine, which can lead to them neglecting key responsibilities that impact other members of the team.

Instead, start with a fresh understanding of each

team member's preferences and continually learn what fulfills, frustrates, and excites them. (Remember Collin in Chapter 3?) Blend these insights with your own observations and assessments, aiming for the sweet spot where team members align with company expectations, enjoy their work, and contribute generously. This strategic placement fosters an environment where creatives exceed expectations, ultimately moving the company toward innovation and increased quality.

GUT CHECK

Are you an active listener?

Have you taken time to develop this skill for yourself and your team?

Do you focus on your team's weaknesses?

Have you created a work environment that encourages open communication?

A Different Approach

As leaders, our goal is to constantly improve how we listen to our teams. The "old school" method of only performing annual reviews creates limitations, especially for creative teams. If you only provide feedback once a year, you miss out on massive opportunities to help your team grow. Annual reviews result in delayed feedback, reducing the chance for quick corrections or timely acknowledgment of achievements. Team members miss out on continuous development and ongoing guidance from leadership. Potential areas for improvement may go unnoticed or unaddressed until the annual review, allowing problems to get worse. Without regular feedback, your team might feel undervalued and unmotivated, leading to decreased performance and engagement. Long gaps between reviews make it challenging to set and adjust goals effectively. This approach can also increase anxiety, as team members may worry about unexpected criticism or having to wait an entire year for recognition.

To enhance your creative culture, consider a more effective approach—one that involves continuous active listening rather than just an annual check-in. At Vers, we rely on these regular, structured meetings to ensure that every voice is heard and that ideas can flow freely.

Weekly 1 on 1's

In order to build a culture of listening and sharing, you have to be committed to communicating with each other frequently. One-on-one meetings might seem like a management nightmare, filled with dull review questions and repetitive structures. However, when they're done right, they can be an absolute game changer. The key is to shift the focus from casual chit-chat to a purposeful, outcome-driven conversation.

In our weekly meetings, the direct report doesn't come prepared with notes and directions. Instead, it's up to the team member to bring opportunities, problems, and self-assessments to the table to drive conversations. This is done by reporting on the highs and lows from the past week, giving updates on projects, and listing specific conversation topics the team member wants to be sure to discuss, as well as listing personal growth actions for themselves, Vers, and our clients. Because the team member is just listing things that are fresh in their minds, prepping usually only takes a few minutes. In the end, the direct report is left with a strong idea of how the team members are doing, how they are contributing to the life of the agency, and specific things they are doing to improve their own skills.

When the team member leads the discussion, an invaluable paradigm shift occurs. It creates a dynamic where junior team members practice leadership skills by running the meeting. This acknowledges that the person doing the job holds valuable insights that their direct report can learn from. By listening and challenging, leaders also cultivate a stronger sense of ownership among the team, leading to faster implementation of improvements and unlocking hidden potential.

Weekly Team Meetings

We extend this culture of listening to our weekly staff meetings, where we try and dispel the myth that creative staff expect leaders to dominate meetings with inspiring speeches. The truth is they value leaders who listen more than they talk. Outside of client and project meetings, our entire team meets twice a week, once on Monday mornings for a staff meeting and again on Wednesday mornings for standup, where we go over the looming projects for the week. Whenever we meet as a full team, my personal goal is to talk for no more than twenty minutes in order to show that every voice matters. While it's true that some vision needs to be presented, it doesn't necessarily have to come solely from the team leader each week.

In order to provide more listening opportunities, we implemented a practice of having other staff members lead a significant part of the meeting every other week. While the weekly meeting structure varies, presentations and highlights are pre-scheduled to ensure purposeful and valuable discussions. This not only breaks down silos but also inspires teams and contributes to a refreshing and dynamic meeting atmosphere.

Quarterly Reviews

At Vers, we conduct reviews at least four times a year. While this frequency might be different for non-creative teams, it has proven effective for our success in fostering a better environment for creatives. Creative individuals benefit from having regular outlets to share their feelings and engage in stimulating conversations within the organization. Given the nature of what their lives look like outside work, understanding their current season—whether rough or smooth—helps tailor the support they need. These quarterly check-ins are essential for maintaining stability during challenging times and providing flexibility during lighter seasons. It's an opportunity to learn about their challenges, growth, and adaptations through different phases.

We assess our creative team's status through a framework derived from Todd Henry's book Herding Tigers. The "stability matrix" provides valuable insight into ensuring that each team member has a balance between challenging work and stability.

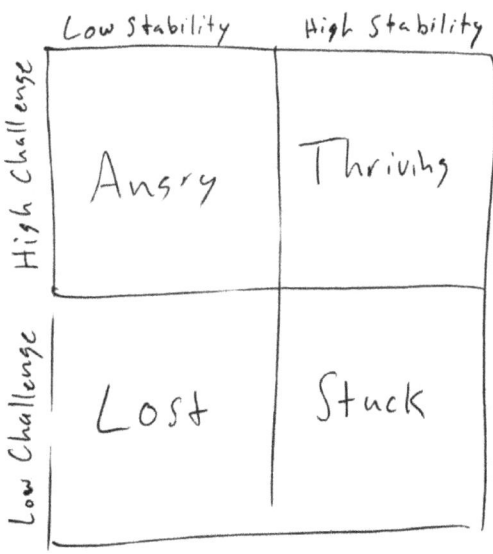

High challenge means clear goals are in place, while high stability indicates motivation and enthusiasm. The matrix is broken into four quadrants. The optimal quadrant we want to see is high challenge/high stability. The burnout zone of high challenge/ low stability can lead to stress and decreased performance. The comfort zone happens in the low challenge/high stability when your team has a stable environment but lacks challenges to push them. The low challenge/low stability area leads to apathy, where your team is disengaged and lacks direction.

During quarterly reviews, we gauge whether our team members feel their current situation is leaning towards lower or higher stability and whether they sense a high- or low-challenge environment. The objective is to create a place where creatives feel both challenged and supported, achieving that perfect balance. Creatives thrive when experiencing high stability supported by leadership and high challenges in their work.

I'm more concerned when someone expresses a sense of low stability than a low challenge because offering more challenge is often a more straightforward fix than addressing stability concerns. Things outside the workplace frequently influence stability. Life is cyclical, and some months are going to be better than others. That's why scheduling these check-in meetings in advance is crucial to establishing a proactive communication pattern. Avoid creating a norm where creatives only check in when issues arise. Traditional questions from annual reviews are still relevant, but consider adding more personalized ones to understand their favorite projects, future excitement, and sources of motivation:

"What are you proud of from the previous quarter?"
"What are you most excited to work on next?"
"What gets you up in the morning?"
"What motivates you?"

Talking about these things can strengthen engagement and give your team members a safe space to share freely.

Quarterly check-ins also enable leaders to discuss upcoming needs and expectations, clarifying the individual's role within the broader project or company objectives. These meetings offer an ideal setting to address concerns like tracking hours and turning potential conflicts into teachable moments. A positive approach turns conversations about improvement into discussions about future victories and personal growth. The goal is to make the employee feel understood, educated, and inspired to overcome challenges.

Effective leaders leverage these quarterly meetings for coaching opportunities rather than focusing on weaknesses. With faster course corrections and increased support, quarterly check-ins contribute to a healthier team dynamic. The emphasis on listening creates a positive environment where individuals feel heard and valued, ultimately saving time, reducing heartaches, and fostering team loyalty.

360 Review

It's easy to spot an unhealthy company culture, especially when employees are leaving for various reasons. To assess our company's well-being, we've added straightforward metrics to our established cues and goals. One key metric we closely monitor is the turnover rate, comparing it year over year. Fortunately, our turnover rate remains significantly below national averages, and I think that is precisely because of these regular check-ins.

A valuable addition to our metrics toolkit is the bi-annual 360 review. This review allows staff members to give feedback on their direct reports, providing insights into how well they feel cared for and valued by their leadership. The survey results offer valuable indicators of organizational improvement over time. By analyzing these results, we can identify areas with lower leadership scores and develop actionable steps to address them.

Foster a Healthy Team Connection

Being a leader who actively listens is like being a counselor. You must be aware of all the dynamics at work in a person's life and how they impact them day-to-day. In a remote work environment, this can be challenging, as you don't always have opportunities for small talk like you do in a traditional office setting. Because of this, I keep an eye on how people are engaging with our company culture, making sure everyone feels connected throughout the day.

To facilitate social connections, we try to create as many opportunities as possible that mix business with pleasure. Our biggest tool for this is Slack. We use Slack all day to talk about clients, projects, and internal communications, but we also use it in a variety of ways that aren't related to work. Our "Dogs of Vers" and "Kids of Vers" channels give people a glimpse into the home life of their coworkers and provide opportunities to celebrate big life events together. And our "Recommendations" and "Pop Culture" channels are a great place to talk about different food, recipes, movies, or TV shows people are watching.

In addition to the constant conversations on Slack, we also host two "Study Halls" each week at the same time and do our best not to schedule client meetings during these windows. These are optional meetings without an agenda where people come to just hang out for a bit. Sometimes, people work while on the call; sometimes, the meetings are used to catch up on quick details related to a project, but more often than not, they're a space for fun. Our staff will frequently save funny stories for Study Hall, and recently a few people on our team have been playing trivia together and posting their scores on Slack.

This creates a sense of community and FOMO for others who want to ensure they're at the next one.

While frequent communication opportunities are essential for a healthy culture, these efforts are often wasted without a strong foundation. At Vers, we have a few guiding philosophies that we use to build an emotionally intelligent team of high performers.

Hire Good People With Shared Values

Our main priority is our client's success, meaning that we always emphasize purpose over profit. Because of this, we prioritize hiring individuals who share our values of being brave, humble, and strategic. This creates a collective commitment throughout the organization to be motivated by communal outcomes, not just personal gain.

Give Our People The Opportunity To Grow

Encouraging the growth of our creative team is paramount. Providing ongoing opportunities for personal and professional development ensures that individuals don't feel stuck in their roles. Whether it involves internal mobility or witnessing organizational progress, we do everything we can to present avenues for continuous growth and new challenges.

Take Care of Good People

Acknowledging good work goes beyond words; it involves tangible care through benefits and pay. At Vers, my commitment is to ensure that the team is well taken care of, which gives a sense of appreciation and fulfillment.

What it All Means

The lesson is clear and simple: If you don't listen to your people, your competition will. We can have all the systems and processes in the world, but if we don't prioritize our team's well-being, they will lose their enthusiasm for the organization and the clients they serve. When we get this right, we maintain a healthy environment. You have to make the time to develop your listening skills to be the most effective leader for your team. With each meeting, one-on-one, and review, you lay a stronger foundation of trust, respect, and support for your team to thrive.

_____
_____
_____

Action Steps

01
Conduct quarterly reviews with team members to provide regular opportunities for open communication, feedback, and coaching. Use these meetings to gauge individual sentiments, address concerns, and align expectations, fostering stability and support within the team.

02
Host weekly staff meetings where listening takes precedence over talking. Allocate time for team members to lead discussions, share insights, and contribute to the meeting agenda, creating a dynamic and inclusive atmosphere.

03
Schedule purpose-driven one-on-one meetings with team members to address specific opportunities, challenges, and performance evaluations. Encourage team members to lead these discussions, fostering ownership, collaboration, and problem-solving within the team.

04
Implement a 360 review to gather feedback from staff members on their direct reports' leadership and support. Analyze the results to identify areas for improvement and develop actionable steps to address them, enhancing organizational effectiveness and employee satisfaction.

05
Actively prioritize the well-being and connection of team members by implementing initiatives that foster a sense of belonging, purpose, and fulfillment.

Chapter 04

CHAPTER

Lie: Standard Operating Procedures (SOPs) ruin great creative work.

Truth: SOPs make great work more consistent.

The Creative Squeeze

When we look at the artists or visionaries that inspire us the most, their groundbreaking ideas are often portrayed as coming from a random spark of creativity. So it feels like a common occurrence that every creative hopes to find their own secret recipe to tap into this mystical "stroke of genius." Early in my career, I was taught the value of creating extensively. I was told not to worry about producing ten perfect pieces of art but rather to work diligently to create thousands in hopes that a few might ultimately turn into masterpieces. We have plenty of examples of these types of prolific creators throughout history, like Vincent van Gogh, who created thousands of paintings in a little over a decade. But despite the volume, which equals a unique piece being produced every 1.5 days, most of us could only name a few of his works. Despite the genius we ascribe to him, we can assume that in order to become this prolific, van Gogh had to have spent time developing efficiencies and processes that helped him have his own creative stroke of genius.

2020 was a tumultuous year for marketing, and I was left questioning whether the industry and creative work would be able to survive the rising technological advancements and the state of our economy. Our team's highly customized, intentional work was expensive, and I knew there would be fewer and fewer people who could afford to pay for this level of service. We tried to think through different ways to switch up our offerings and pricing, but it didn't feel like it would be worth it to our clients. Meanwhile, our expenses continued to rise with inflation while profits continued to decline.

After two years of stagnation, I was fortunate enough to go on a retreat with a handful of agency owners who did the same type of work that I did. It was here that I met the founder of an agency with over 500 employees working across 70 different industries and a revenue stream of over $75 million a year. He was gracious enough to open up his books, showing me his team structure, sales strategies, and how his business operated on a massive scale doing the same work we did. Like Vers, they had good leaders, good vision, and did quality work. However I quickly noticed the biggest gap was in their detailed and organized standard operating procedures.

It started with their hiring and onboarding processes, which took narrow job descriptions with different creative disciplines and tied them to broader organizational goals. They had a detailed sales process that worked to engage potential clients while also vetting them to ensure long-term partnerships. There was a process for every single service they sold that was built out like a product in a factory, with a digital conveyor assembly for marketing and creative projects that they could easily tailor to each client. When I started my career, I saw clear paths to growing us to a medium-sized agency, but creating something bigger than myself that could bring lasting value to clients felt like a mystery. After seeing his agency's SOPs, I was beginning to envision how it was possible to maximize a creative team in order to bring the most value possible.

The Creative Squeeze

For most creative leaders, building out these conveyor belts to become more efficient sounds like a nightmare. As inspiring as it was to see how this agency worked, I knew that it wasn't realistic to build carbon copies of everything at Vers. However, I discovered there were processes we needed to put into place in order to set Vers up for the best possible future. The lesson I learned was that your team will always perform their best when they are given the most amount of clarity possible. Clarity creates accountability and helps team members aim their creative energy at the right goals. I've heard several times from creatives that they don't want to work from a template and want the freedom to go where their ideas take them. But as a leader, we often have to help let go of the idea that creating something new is always within our scope.

The longer I've worked in this industry I've come to realize that creative work is most often a process of copying some version of something that has already been made. This is the opposite of how we usually think about art, where structures and systems are often seen as the antithesis of expression, stifling the freedom to create from scratch. It's all about changing the creative mindset in order to make a bigger impact. It's not as if implementing processes takes away the opportunity to create something new. Instead, it means that channeling your creativity into making a template has the potential to reach thousands of people instead of just a few. Unique and innovative processes are scalable and have a value that goes well beyond individual projects. Effective leadership is about looking at the big picture and determining how to make the biggest impact possible. The creative industry's embrace of digitization has made these efforts easier than ever, and now your best work can be the systems, processes, notes, and templates developed with your team to consistently knock it out of the park.

> **UNIQUE AND INNOVATIVE PROCESSES ARE SCALABLE. THEIR VALUE TRANSCENDS INDIVIDUAL PROJECTS**

Whether your team has an annual budget of $3 million and is filled with director-level positions, or you're a smaller organization where a few people are wearing multiple hats, implementing written processes for each task can supercharge your organization's efficiency. In my experience with graphic design for branding and campaign art, I initially started each project from scratch. I believed using templates or processes would result in dull and repetitive work. However, after completing around 500 projects, I realized I had unconsciously developed my own processes. While I didn't recognize it as a template then, I was consistently following the same steps that could be systematized for greater efficiency.

GUT CHECK

Do you believe in the power of a template?

What are the 3 things you and your team spend the most amount of time doing?

What are the most repeatable things you do?

Can you bring clarity to those things with a check list that will make them more efficient or better quality?

(HINT: A great place to start is your calendar, regular deliverables, meeting notes, and agendas. Build a process to get the most out of that time. Meetings are costing way more money than you want to admit!)

The Process Pathway

Life at a nonprofit is typically pretty cyclical. There are annual donor strategies that are often focused on events, as well as weekly and monthly touchpoints where different people within the organization nurture leads. Although much of this is tied to the calendar, each project requires a massive amount of effort from your team. Each step builds towards the formidable annual report, where the organization gets a snapshot of how your team has been spending its time. In my decades of working with nonprofits, I've seen countless organizations approach the annual report as just that, a report, instead of looking at it as a blueprint for change. This type of data is the perfect time to evaluate if your organization is allocating its time and resources in the most effective way possible.

Nonprofit budgets are constantly changing, and the process of allocating funds is always a challenge. We often hear staff members saying that the organization needs to hire more people, but we rarely think about intentionally building our systems to improve the return on our investments. The same mindset for developing process documents in creative work applies to organizational development. A strong SOP should start with the goals that the organization is trying to accomplish and include language that describes the accountability of what is expected from the team. Remember, accountability is not judgment; it's about organizing follow through, not deciding if an event was successful or not.

Life inside a church is similarly cyclical. After all, Easter and Christmas come at the same time every year. During my 12 years working inside the church, I never once saw an SOP. That's crazy, especially when you consider that the average church allocates about 70% of its resources to building and producing a weekly event every Sunday. Successful churches are always looking for ways to shake things up and stand out, but the reality is a year inside a church consists of 48 productions that are similar, 4 special productions, and 2 or 3 seasons of midweek small group meetings. There is perhaps no other type of organization that should have their work templatized as much as churches should. Despite this, even the biggest churches start from scratch for every design asset for sermon series, open blank video timelines, and recreate live production elements, all in an attempt to pursue a stroke of genius.

What has proven successful for my team was creating an organizational mindset about the importance of automating steps, creating clear checklists, setting time boundaries, and incorporating the questions I ask as a creative director into our processes. While templates remain flexible, this approach saves time, minimizes errors, and prevents the inadvertent omission of crucial steps. The task itself may seem tedious, especially with multiple departments and specialized team members, but these processes ensure everyone knows and meets your expectations efficiently.

While this book isn't trying to impose challenging steps that generate more work, I want to acknowledge that implementing processes requires an investment of time and occasionally saying no to other opportunities. But by committing yourself to building scalable processes, you'll ultimately create a more efficient, streamlined workflow that will save time and resources in the long run. Until the other agency owner showed me their processes, I couldn't begin to wrap my head around what would be beneficial and what would be more busy work. So I hope by sharing some of our processes I can do the same for you. If nothing else you can look at them and compare them to your own and pat yourself on the back that you're doing better than us! Below, I will provide a brief overview of three processes that have become essential to our agency. Scan the QR code to access the rest of the documents.

Intake/Discovery Process

Before we start any creative project, we need to do our homework on the organization we're working with. To begin, we dive into each organization's target audience in order to better understand who is on the other side of their communication. We need to know who these people are, what they want in an interaction with the organization, and what specific pain points they might be bringing to the table. From there, we establish the values that the brand is bringing to the table. This involves identifying their core principles and unique value propositions that differentiate them as an organization.

Next we analyze the competitive landscape to see how similar organizations are positioning themselves. This helps us begin to craft a strategy that stands out and avoids redundancy. We look at what competitors are doing well and where there are gaps that our clients can fill. This analysis not only helps provide a comprehensive view of the market but it also informs the creative decisions we will make when we start to build out the campaign.

Campaign Process

Our campaign process covers the intake, planning, and execution of the proposed work we will be doing for clients. Even though each client is unique, the same overarching questions apply to each, and we want to be sure to have answers to specific questions that will shape the scope of work and set expectations for our team and the organization we're working with. We need to know the overarching goal of the campaign, the budget and timeline we have to work with, and any potential limitations that could get in the way of reaching the goal. We also identify the key performance indicators (KPIs) and what the expected return on investment (ROI) will be in order to accurately measure the success of the campaign.

From there, we plan a strategy that aligns with the client's objectives, resources, and target audience. This includes developing the creative concepts and determining where they will ultimately be hosted. After we turn ideas

Chapter 05

into assets, we do a last run-through to ensure that everything is in place and meets our standards before we shift into monitoring and reporting mode.

Reporting Process

Once the goals are determined and the assets are created, we can actively evaluate their success based on the KPIs that were established earlier. Vers takes a ton of pride in doing great reporting for a variety of reasons. First, it helps provide transparency and accountability, allowing all stakeholders to see how campaigns are performing in relation to the set objectives. This creates a visibility that ensures everyone is on the same page and can make informed decisions. Second, consistent and detailed reporting helps identify what is working well and what isn't. By analyzing the data collected through KPIs, we can pinpoint areas of success to replicate in the future and areas of improvement to address quickly. We aim to establish a continuous feedback loop in order to constantly work towards better outcomes.

Third, a strong reporting process allows us to measure the ROI accurately. Understanding the financial impact of the campaign helps us better set future budgets internally and demonstrate the value of our efforts to our clients externally. Lastly, comprehensive reporting contributes to our culture of learning and improvement. By documenting insights and outcomes, we build a database of knowledge we can go back and learn from any time we want.

Rhythm to Scale

We streamline our processes using project management software. When beginning a project, all necessary steps are present in the base project template—a tried-and-true framework that significantly enhances our chances of success. If a project has unique aspects or requires adjustments for an ongoing campaign, we make specific changes while benefiting from the solid foundation provided by the template. But what about those larger projects that aren't repetitive and fall outside your regular workflow? Those can absolutely be streamlined as well.

Making templates for larger, one-off projects

similarly begins with writing out all the steps, possible timelines, checkpoints with key decision makers, and the clear goals you're working towards. Then we find really strong examples of finished work that is as close as possible to the desired work in order to create a mood board or descriptive example in order to show what the project should and should not be. A basic outline where you plug all of the variables for the work, sets checks and balances, timelines, budgets, and samples that can help both parties agree upon details already seems like a template, doesn't it?

If all of this seems easy enough, then why doesn't everyone already do it? The answer is that most good project managers and creative directors are good precisely because they do this well. It may just be in their heads, not in a formal step-by-step document shared on a drive for the whole team to use. I've seen plenty of successful creatives say that they can't do a particular project without applying this type of process at the forefront. Of course, it's true that they could do it, but it will almost always take longer, be more frustrating, and result in a substandard outcome. The reality is that if we don't take the time to create a template, thoroughly analyze challenges, and understand all communication requirements, we're left with two options:

Option 1 is to overcharge for the work to create a buffer for potential roadblocks, ultimately creating less overall value for the work.

Option 2 is to fail.

The Creative Squeeze

A while back, I set out to work with an extremely creative builder who was talented, believed in his ability to get things done inexpensively, and was excited to add my design to his portfolio. After months of trying to get him to lay out the project and put realistic timelines and budgets in place so I could evaluate whether it was worth it, I finally had to take it on myself. It was easier for me to stand my ground on this because the house was for me and my family. Failure could not be an option, and I wasn't about to run out of money before it was finished. I needed to understand how the process was going to look before it ever started in order to fully know what was possible and what success would look like within the timeline and budget.

One of my favorite things to watch is a British TV show called Grand Designs. There are over 20 seasons featuring some of the most incredible custom homes I've ever seen. Some of the homes are large, some of them are small, some are luxurious, and some are down to earth. But no matter what type of home it is, a common theme in every episode is that the projects always seem to cost nearly double the time and budget they initially projected. This isn't always because of a lack of detailed processes. Some of the projects and construction took so long because that was the only way people could afford them; others had additions to the family that caused a change in plans. Luckily, most of us don't have to budget and scope out projects that take a decade to complete. But clients experience this same sort of phenomenon where changes need to be made on the fly. So making every effort we can to account for every single detail on a project with as much expertise as possible is in everyone's best interest.

The truth is that people who don't want to plan, template, budget, and take time to clearly communicate all of the expectations of a project are not good collaborators. They're most often the type of person who is difficult to work with and will end up frustrating your team. In my experience, this type of person usually isn't even that happy with the final product that you painstakingly put together despite the lack of structure. The best way to handle this type of person is to tell them the truth: say no. Don't take their money, and invest your time into a different project that can be set up for success from the start.

Starting a creative project is one thing, but finishing it on time and on budget requires an insane amount of discipline. This skill set often evades me and most of my creative colleagues. That's why we need these planned-out processes and project managers (a position that might as well be called "accountability partners"…or "adult babysitters") to help us combat the creative desire to feed the lie that more time and budget will make a better final product.

BONUS GUT CHECK

Do you stop and consider what doing something new will cost?

Do you care about your team's success enough to say no to unplanned work?

Are you asking your team to pull off miracles with unrealistic timelines, unclear budgets, and lack of clarity? If so, start by acknowledging it with them and put SOP documents in place!

What It All Means

Creative work carries the reputation of being unbound and free, allowing our imaginations to pursue different ideas without restraint. But the truth is that the best work requires a systematic approach that blends creativity with structure. This balance ensures that innovative ideas are not only generated but also effectively executed and refined. A structured process provides the framework within which creativity can thrive, offering clear goals, deadlines, and criteria for success.

Action Steps

01
Take a look at your calendar and project lists and lay out all of the projects that you and your team do regularly.

02
Go through each project and define the goals and parameters upfront. Answer all of the key questions regarding the project scope, timeline, and client approval process.

03
Identify and communicate potential obstacles or risks. Do this with every team member who is involved in the project to foster a culture of proactive problem-solving and risk mitigation.

04
Create detailed project guides outlining the necessary steps. Utilize accessible online platforms or internal documentation systems so everyone on your team can access them.

05
Before taking on a new project, talk to someone who is an expert or has the most amount of experience in that type of work. Always budget double what you think it will take the first time. Worst case scenario, you have some extra budget left over that you can use to make a process document for the next time you have to do a similar project.

CHAPTER

Lie: Growth means you should always be doing more.

Truth: Growth comes from doing the right things, not more things.

It's fair to say that all creative work is a matter of navigating complexities. Whether you're a graphic designer, videographer, or copywriter, you constantly face the challenge of transforming abstract ideas into tangible outputs that effectively communicate a message. Regardless of the discipline, the process demands an intricate understanding of both the medium and the message, ensuring that the final product resonates with the intended audience while meeting the strategic goal of communicating the complexities of the message. I would never go as far as saying that this process is easy. However, the challenges with creative communication are typically artistic in nature and have to do with balancing nuance, aesthetics, and clarity to produce work that is both engaging and impactful.

Being a creative leader means taking on a role where solutions are rarely straightforward. Whereas creative work is responsible for communicating complexities, creative leadership is responsible for solving them. It's not just about making artistic decisions, it's about making strategic ones. Creative leaders must guide their teams through ambiguity, identify and remove obstacles, and foster an environment that encourages innovation and resilience. They need to align the team's creative efforts with the organization's broader objectives, ensuring that the work not only communicates effectively but also drives strategic outcomes. This involves inspiring and motivating the team, setting a clear vision, and making decisions that balance creativity with practical constraints. Each one of these steps involves prioritizing strategic structures that work to remove obstacles and demotivators in order for a creative team to perform at their best. But oftentimes, three major obstacles stand in the way.

The first is that taking on a leadership role can feel like a creative downgrade. For someone who is transitioning from full-time creative work into leadership, it can feel like trading off something that is fun and gives you life, to something boring and monotonous. It's important to recognize that this shift doesn't mean stepping away from creative problem-solving; rather, it involves applying creativity on a larger scale. For leaders who are inherently creative, this broader scope can be highly motivating, offering new opportunities to innovate and make a significant impact within the organization.

> **IT'S NOT JUST ABOUT MAKING ARTISTIC DECISIONS, IT'S ABOUT MAKING STRATEGIC ONES.**

The second challenge involves learning to work with other types of leaders. When a creative person takes on a leadership role, they oftentimes transition from being around other creatives to being around people who have a whole different set of skills and lack creative vision. People who are not creative thinkers often create roadblocks because their managerial mindset makes them apprehensive about change. They may struggle to embrace innovative ideas, leading to obstacles that hinder progress. This lack of creative thinking can result in resistance to new approaches and an adherence to the status quo, which can be frustrating for those who thrive on creativity and innovation.

The third challenge has to do with an inability to look holistically at the organization. Creative thinkers tend to move fast, and stay focused on the ones working closest with them on a project. We tend to implement specific tools and processes and assume that everyone else should follow our lead and have the same excitement for innovation that we do. While this idea is well-intentioned and backed by good know-how, it overlooks the broader implications for the entire organization. Implementing such changes requires considering factors like timing, resource allocation, and overall impact, which often need to be accounted for when thinking solely within departmental boundaries.

At each of these potential roadblocks comes the temptation to simply take on more work. But that will only ever lead to burnout and diminish the quality of both your leadership and creative output. Instead, the focus should be on strategic thinking that prioritizes focusing on the right opportunities that will move your team forward faster. Creatively, it's not all that different from sitting down at a specific project. You still need inspiration, and a strategic path to get where you want to go. Challenges encountered in leadership are still a creative problem to be solved, they just take place on a higher level.

GUT CHECK

Do you operate under the belief that doing more will produce better results?

Do you think of leadership as a creative pursuit?

Are you putting off assuming more responsibility because you fear it will be a creative downgrade?

When facing a problem, is your default setting to take on more work?

Do you look for ways to collaborate with other leaders who lack a creative vision?

Plotting Your Path

Transitioning from simply adding more to your plate to working strategically on the right things requires a shift in mindset and approach. Instead of piling on tasks, it's about focusing on reigning your instincts into actionable and innovative solutions and learning to de-risk and experiment in order to build resilient strategies that can adapt to change. By balancing creative thinking with rigorous analysis, you can uncover breakthrough ideas and develop sustainable solutions. A strong strategic approach not only enhances productivity but also ensures that your efforts are directed toward activities that drive meaningful progress and long-term success. And the best part is that it can be a team sport.

When encountering a complex problem, good leaders rely on the strong team they've built. Get around a table with a big whiteboard, and begin to work through actionable steps that build toward a resolution.

Clearly Define the Problem

Gather the team to discuss and identify the key barriers to overcome and any potential boundaries you need to work within to understand its scope fully. Ensure that everyone has a shared understanding of the problem and its complexities.

Brainstorm Solutions

Encourage the team to generate as many ideas as possible. It's crucial to create a judgment-free zone where no idea is easily dismissed. Set a specific time limit for the brainstorming session to remain focused, and use tools like mind mapping to visualize and organize ideas.

Vote on Ideas

Review all the ideas that have been generated and allow each member to vote on the paths that they think have the most potential. Discuss the results of the votes to ensure clarity and consensus on the best ideas. Then take the top three ideas and rank them one through three.

Create Actionable Steps

Develop detailed and actionable steps for the top three ideas. Assign responsibilities and deadlines for each action step, identify any potential obstacles and make a plan for how to address them. Document the action plan to eliminate any confusion that team members might have about their roles.

Schedule Routine Check-Ins

Set regular meetings to review progress on the action steps. Use these check-ins to discuss any challenges, adjust plans as needed, and maintain momentum. Track progress and celebrate small wins to help keep the team motivated.

Evaluate and Report

Once the project is complete, conduct a thorough evaluation of the outcomes. Compare the results against the initial goals and expectations, and document any lessons learned or areas for improvement. Prepare a report to share with stakeholders that highlights successes and insights gained from the project.

All of this might seem fairly elementary and maybe even a little inefficient. After all, you're potentially taking a full team away from other tasks and responsibilities that they need to be working on. But there really is no shortcut for this type of high-level strategic thinking. AI can give ideas and organize thoughts and next steps quickly, but there is something about the buy-in when a team devotes time and puts the work in to make it through a complex problem that is difficult to outsource to technology. There also seems to be a level of humility that comes with following a simple process like this that we often want to skip. But you have to trust the process.

Efficiency Over Effort

In your organization, what defines progress? How do you measure growth? For many leaders, it's the visible presence of people at their desks, diligently working longer hours, and ticking off more tasks. They believe that getting things done is the biggest signifier of success, but that's not a realistic way to measure anything. The true challenge lies not in adding more tasks to your creative team's plate but in guiding them with purpose. It's about identifying and focusing on the right tasks that drive meaningful outcomes and inspire innovation.

In my experience working with various companies, big and small, a common issue I've seen is the lack of clear growth metrics for team members and even entire teams. Without defining the most valuable contributions, we often mistake visible busyness for real productivity. The strongest way to set your high-performers up for measurable success is to grant them permission to stop doing less valuable tasks. As the leader, this involves protecting them from activities that don't propel the team closer to their goals or contribute meaningfully to the overall organization. Granting your team the freedom to stop doing these things will significantly enhance their productivity and make them enjoy the work more.

I have watched countless organizations operate under the mentality of doing more of everything, thinking this was the safest way to lead their team. Admittedly, this was my thought process for years. I continuously added more to overflowing plates, pushed more goals, and pressured my team to complete more tasks to move Vers forward. During this time, I failed to create a healthy environment for my team to feel safe enough not only to push back but also to communicate their bandwidth with me. It took me stepping back and evaluating myself to realize what I was doing. Through this process, I learned how to give my team the freedom to validate their needs, share their perspectives on workload, and communicate when they have reached their limits.

> **YOU MUST IDENTIFY AND FOCUS ON TASKS THAT DRIVE MEANINGFUL OUTCOMES AND INSPIRE INNOVATION**

Doing this opened the door to now being able to have regular conversations where every team member feels safe enough to call out what they see is not working, how to fix the issue, and even speak into what they have to say 'no' to. Hearing this directly from the people working on the projects then allows me to measure which tasks are actually valuable for our clients, for our creative process, and for the overall health of my team. This is how you build trust with your team. This is how you can squeeze more out of your creatives.

So how do you know which tasks to stop? It's all about learning to assess value.

The Value Paradox

Imagine you're in the batter's box against a Major League Baseball pitcher. The crowd is loud, the lights are bright, and you're gripping the bat tight, trying to guess what sort of pitch he's going to throw. While for most of us, the scenario would probably be entertaining to watch, the reality is that very few of us would make contact, let alone get a hit.

We do something similar to our internal teams all the time. We throw major league challenges at them without providing the adequate resources, training, or experiences they need to be successful. This oversight can have significant costs for the organization as the team needs help to bridge the gap between the expected and actual value of the project. The result is not a professional outcome, and the team ends up investing more effort than necessary for the project's value.

One of the most crucial parts of being a strategist is understanding the value of an outcome. Whenever you strategize and plan, it's essential to ask yourself three simple questions:

1. What is the best possible outcome worth to your organization?
2. What is the cost of your proposed solution to your organization?
3. What can be done to bridge the gap so the organization gets the best possible outcome?

These types of questions help you transition into a value-based plan, not to be confused with a values-based plan. Values are an essential part of making decisions. They're how we view the world and intuitively know when a particular situation aligns or conflicts with our core beliefs. But they're not the only metric used to judge a decision. As a leader, your decisions are a constant battle between value and values. While values help us see the potential in a particular idea, value helps us determine if it's possible. This distinction is where a lot of creative ideators struggle. They are able to see the potential but cannot judge whether all of the necessary resources are there. Approaching problems through the lens of value is oftentimes the easiest and most effective way to make a decision.

Recently I was having a conversation with one of our creative staff leaders who had been navigating work with a potential client. This organization needed a substantial amount of work— strategy, branding, web development, communications, a building campaign, and internal training. All together we were talking about well over $100,000 worth of services that Vers could provide to push them forward. The client recognized our expertise and was eager to get started, but with so many potential paths, we had to prioritize their immediate needs and identify the best entry point for our collaboration. We needed to identify what would bring them the most value and prioritize our efforts to ensure we could effectively address their most pressing challenges and set the stage for future success. Unless both sides fully understand what we have to work with, what it's going to cost, and how the outcome compares with other potential options, it's impossible to succeed.

Chapter 06

Roadblocks and Sacred Cows

On paper, making strategic decisions based on value seems simple. But in reality, the process is often filled with complexities, particularly for those who have been at the same organization for a significant amount of time and have been indoctrinated in two of the most cancerous threats to growth: roadblocks and sacred cows. Sacred cows need no introduction and are likely the first thing that comes to mind when considering the least valuable tasks that you or your team do regularly. These practices persist because they are understood to be untouchable and are often instituted by well-meaning boards, leaders, or donors without considering the time, resources, and long-term consequences. As circumstances change, these practices often make little sense but remain simply out of habit. Most organizations are eager to implement new initiatives but struggle to let go of outdated ones.

To work towards eliminating sacred cows, you must first understand their value and weigh it against the emotional investment they carry. Evaluate your own emotional equity to determine if you have enough 'in the bank' to challenge these practices. A common mistake is failing to fully understand the value of the sacred cow and the perspectives of all stakeholders, leading to one-sided decisions that can cause more harm than good. Begin by evaluating whether the sacred cow makes sense within a strategic value framework. Investigate its origins and understand all key stakeholders' views. Do not consider your research complete until you have heard confirming statements from multiple parties, especially those from diverse groups within the organization. This thorough approach increases the likelihood of accurately assessing the sacred cow and making informed, strategic decisions that benefit the organization.

Compared to sacred cows, roadblocks are a little scarier and often more emotionally complex. Simply put, roadblocks are processes or people that stop progress and forward momentum and often stem from a deep-seated pain where someone has previously tried something and failed. Unlike sacred cows, which are entrenched practices that need to be eliminated, roadblocks are hurdles that prevent the implementation of new, valuable growth strategies. These roadblocks often come from well-meaning individuals but can be detrimental to good ideas or strategies. Understanding who is likely to block your ideas and why is crucial when presenting your value proposition. If you can grasp the context for someone's opposition to your proposal, you can proactively address their concerns and demonstrate why your idea is worth pursuing despite potential opposition.

One tactical skill to develop is the ability to anticipate roadblocks, a competence that comes more easily to those with higher emotional intelligence. Avoid introducing ideas or strategies in planned meetings as if they are some grand part of your intellectual property.

Instead, be relational, and bring things up in one-on-one conversations positioning ideas with intrigue as opposed to a declaration. Don't hold on to your ideas so closely, and be willing to make adjustments based on the feedback you receive. When we're too attached to an idea, we tend to get defensive and are unable to hear valuable input that gives other members of your team ownership. Keep a loose grip, and be ready to modify as needed. Lastly, seek out conversations with the decision-makers who will be affected by your idea. Ask how implementing your idea might impact them or others, whether it would make things worse, or if they foresee any potential opposition. By being flexible with how you approach a potential change, you open the door for more honest feedback and collaboration.

When dealing with roadblocks it's essential to remember that people are generally opposed to change. While they may not express it openly, resistance is a common reaction to anything new or different. Anticipate this opposition and make a plan to work through it. I can't even begin to name how many times I've revealed an idea too passionately and as a result, encountered unexpected resistance that could have been avoided with a more measured approach. By introducing ideas with intrigue rather than certainty, remaining open to adjustments, and seeking diverse feedback, you can better navigate roadblocks. This not only helps to minimize opposition but also fosters a collaborative environment where innovative ideas can thrive despite initial resistance.

What It All Means

Real progress within your organization comes not from doing more but from strategically prioritizing the right tasks. It's necessary to spend time reevaluating how you measure growth and success. You can foster an environment where your team thrives by identifying and focusing on tasks that truly matter. It's about granting your team the freedom to say no to less valuable activities and protecting them from unnecessary demands. As leaders, it's up to us to foster open communication, listen to our team's feedback, and use these insights to drive meaningful change. Embrace this approach, and you'll not only enhance productivity but also build a more engaged, innovative, and resilient team.

_____

_____

_____

Action Steps

01
Define meaningful progress metrics that go beyond mere busyness and focus on strategic productivity.

02
Grant top performers permission to delegate or discontinue tasks that don't align with team goals.

03
Facilitate discussions to align team members on project value and resource allocation. Define which tasks are essential for achieving organizational objectives and which can be deprioritized.

04
Identify and challenge common unhealthy habits such as non-budgeted collaboration, iterations, and unrealistic expectations.

05
Encourage calculated risk-taking by evaluating the worth of risks in relation to desired outcomes.

CHAPTER

Lie: Guiding principles are corporate B.S.

Truth: Guiding principles are the backbone of your organization.

Principles and values—you probably have them within your organization. You may even have some idea of what they are. And if you have them committed to memory, you're really on top of your game. But having a list of values on a random landing page and relying on those values to help inform decisions and lead your organization are two very different things. When your core values are genuinely lived and breathed, they provide a clear compass for navigating complex landscapes and making decisions that align with your core mission.

For most creatives, guiding principles are the cornerstone of all corporate mumbo jumbo spewed by blubbering idiots at the yearly Christmas party. They see these values as empty rhetoric, a series of buzzwords strung together to satisfy a company checklist before they were ever hired. And who can blame them? Take a second and think about all of the places you've ever worked. Chances are, nearly all of them had guiding principles that someone at some point took the time to carefully write. But how many of them can you actually remember?

While it's true that guiding principles often fail to make a connection, the reality is that your organization's mission statement, guiding principles, and core values work together to define the company's identity, purpose, and ethical framework. They provide a cohesive direction for your actions, decision-making, and culture. With these firmly in place, your team will be aligned in pursuit of your organization's goals.

The key to transforming these principles from mere words to lived experiences lies in integrating them into every facet of your organization. This means incorporating your values into performance reviews, using them as benchmarks for hiring, and referencing them in day-to-day decision-making. When a team sees its leaders making decisions based on core values, it reinforces their importance and fosters a culture of integrity and consistency. It takes words off the page and makes them visible every day in the organization's actions. But staying centered on guiding principles is easier said than done.

GUT CHECK

Have you defined your organization's guiding principles?

What is your relationship to the company's values?

Does your team know the organization's principles and why they were chosen?

Do your mission statement and your guiding values help your team perform better on a day-to-day basis?

Why Values Matter

As leaders, it may feel like we don't have time to think about values and guiding principles. However, neglecting them can lead to a lot of time wasted on poor decisions. If your principles are vague and irrelevant—crafted hastily during a one-day leadership session years ago to check a box for an executive training exercise or to appease the board—it's time for a change. Making decisions becomes even more challenging when your mission statement is so generic that it could apply to any number of organizations. What's needed is an elevated approach. One that ensures that your values and principles are clear, relevant, and specific to your mission so they can genuinely guide your team's actions.

> **STOP VIEWING VALUES AS MERE WORDS. RECOGNIZE THE REAL VALUE THAT COMES FROM A TEAM UNIFIED IN MISSION**

Guiding principles, core values, and mission statements all fall in the same problematic bucket for organizations. While it seems small compared to all of the other things an organization is dealing with, it becomes a significant issue because it's challenging for an organization to make cohesive, brand-wide decisions when everyone interprets the values differently. By better aligning your creatives with organizational clarity, you can enhance their productivity and effectiveness. Clearly defined guiding principles form the backbone of everything an organization does, from daily operations to long-term strategies. As a leader, it's crucial to stop viewing values as mere words and start recognizing the real value that comes from having a team united by a shared mission. Understanding why guiding principles are important is the first step toward leveraging their full potential.

Consistency and Coherence

Guiding principles help maintain consistency and coherence across all projects and interactions. They serve as a steady foundation upon which all organizational activities are built, ensuring that every action, decision, and communication aligns with shared core values. This alignment is crucial for strengthening your organization's overall brand identity, as it guarantees that the team consistently reinforces the same image and reputation in everything they do.

Think of guiding principles as the first step in quality control. Just as a well-defined set of standards ensures that products meet specific criteria regardless of who manufactures them, guiding principles ensure that the quality of your team's work remains high and consistent, no matter who is involved in the project. This consistency builds trust with your audience and allows them to have high expectations met.

Decision-Making Framework

When it comes to making decisions, having a clear set of guiding principles is invaluable. Your principles provide a roadmap that offers clarity and efficiency, allowing you and your team to streamline the decision-making process. By aligning potential choices with established core values and long-term goals, your team can ensure that every decision supports the overarching mission and vision. Instead of getting bogged down by uncertainty and conflicting priorities, decision-makers can quickly assess options against established values. This alignment simplifies the decision-making process, enabling your team to make quicker, more confident decisions that keep things moving forward.

This framework doesn't just help with individual team members making decisions. Guiding principles work to foster a unified approach to decision-making across an entire organization. When everyone understands and adheres to the same set of values, it reduces discrepancies across an organization. This shared understanding ensures that decisions made at all levels of the organization are consistent and support the same strategic objectives. It also enhances accountability, allowing team members to justify their decisions by referencing connections to core values. Guiding principles help individuals make informed decisions with confidence, knowing they are aligned with the organization's standards and long-term vision.

Client Trust and Relationships

For our clients, guiding principles are crucial for building trust and fostering strong relationships. These principles act as a tool for transparent communication, clearly conveying your organization's standards. When clients understand your guiding principles, they get a clear insight into your organization's approach, process, and the quality of the work you do, setting clear expectations from the outset.

Clear guiding principles are also one of the easiest ways to differentiate your organization from its competitors. In a crowded marketplace, having a clear and consistent set of values sets you apart, showing your audience that you stand for something more significant than surface-level engagement. It signals that you are dedicated to maintaining a high level of quality and can play a major role in solidifying relationships. When clients see your guiding principles reflected in your work, it reinforces their confidence that you deliver on promises.

Team Alignment and Culture

Guiding principles serve as a unifying force that has the ability to rally everyone around a shared vision. They work to create a strong organizational culture that helps provide a team with a clear sense of purpose and direction. When team members understand and believe in a set of core values, it fosters a deep sense of belonging and commitment to the collective mission. It helps them understand the standards and values that are valued and expected, allows new employees to integrate smoothly, and aligns everyone's efforts around common goals.

It might sound corny, but clear guiding principles also boost motivation and morale for a team. Team members who feel connected to their organization's values are more likely to be engaged and enthusiastic about their work. This connection instills a sense of pride and loyalty, making your team feel that their contributions are meaningful and appreciated. As a result, your team is happier and more connected.

Innovation and Creativity

While it might seem like principles would limit creativity, they actually do the opposite. Principles provide the right boundaries for creativity to thrive by encouraging a culture of experimentation and healthy risk-taking. When team members feel security in established values, they feel empowered to push boundaries and think outside the box, and can be confident that their ideas will be supported because they are linked to these values.

Having a strong grasp of core values helps foster collaboration and cross-pollination of ideas. When everyone is guided by the same principles, it creates a common language and shared understanding that facilitates better communication and teamwork. This creates a collaborative environment that is a fertile ground for creativity as diverse perspectives come together to generate breakthrough ideas. Established guiding principles also ensure that new ideas and strategies maintain the integrity and consistency of the brand. As innovation happens, it's done with a clear sense of the organization's identity, ensuring that creative solutions enhance rather than dilute the brand's reputation.

> **PRINCIPLES PROVIDE THE RIGHT BOUNDARIES FOR CREATIVITY TO THRIVE**

Adaptability and Growth

As our agency has grown, guiding principles have been essential for helping us scale seamlessly. They ensure that new team members and departments align with our established culture and values and create a cohesive and unified team. By embedding these principles into the onboarding process, we are able to quickly integrate new hires, ensuring that everyone, regardless of their role or location, operates with the same foundational values. This alignment has been crucial for maintaining a consistent culture and operational approach as we expand.

In a fast-evolving industry, change is constant, and the ability to adapt is crucial for sustainability and relevance. Whether we are entering new markets, adopting new technologies, or restructuring departments, these principles ensure that our decisions and actions remain true to our mission and values. This stability allows us to navigate uncertainty with confidence, knowing that our core identity is preserved. When faced with industry shifts or unexpected challenges, these principles encourage us to embrace change rather than resist it. They provide a framework for evaluating new opportunities and making strategic decisions that are aligned with our long-term goals. This adaptability is essential for innovation and continuous improvement, enabling us to stay ahead of the curve and capitalize on emerging trends.

Ethical and Social Responsibility

Ultimately, our guiding principles are about how you treat others. They help ensure that our work is not only creative and innovative but also responsible and respectful. For some, this means compliance with specific regulations, but for most, it involves actively seeking ways to make a positive impact. This commitment to a positive impact extends beyond your immediate organizational goals; it encompasses our interactions with clients, partners, employees, and the broader community.

Adhering to ethical guiding principles in your operations also strengthens your reputation and builds trust with the public. In today's world, your audience is increasingly conscious of the ethical implications of their choices. They want to engage with organizations that demonstrate a genuine commitment to the things they care about and the causes they support. Explicitly spelling out what you believe in helps enhance credibility and foster loyalty.

Applying the Principles

When I first started Vers, I knew that I didn't want it to be just another agency. I wanted us to stand for something and do work that made a meaningful impact. Because of this, I knew that having a clear vision and mission was essential, but I wasn't sure how to establish it clearly. I spent time looking at other organizations that inspired me, making notes about their values and how they were lived out in their work. From there, I brought in the team to get their thoughts. Having the staff work together to refine our core values was a strategic move on my part to ensure every single person was on board with what we were trying to accomplish. I wanted the principles we chose to mean something to the team, so I did everything I could to foster a sense of ownership.

I remember standing in front of my team, overwhelmed with the feeling that what we were doing would truly shape the future of Vers. We had intentional conversations and dug deep to uncover what really mattered to us as individuals and as a collective. Each team member brought their unique perspective, and together, we explored our motivations, aspirations, and the kind of impact we wanted to make. For hours, we discussed our experiences, values, and visions for the future. We challenged each other to think beyond the obvious, to question our assumptions, and to articulate what made us passionate about our work. It was a process of self-discovery and mutual understanding, one that required honesty, vulnerability, and a willingness to listen.

I wrote everyone's thoughts up on the whiteboard and we worked together for two days to define three core values that truly embody who we are. As we sifted through these ideas, certain themes began to emerge. We noticed a strong emphasis on mission, the drive to innovate, and a deep-seated desire to make a positive difference in the world. These values, deeply embedded in our DNA, are acknowledged daily and contribute to a culture that extends beyond individual projects:

Humble

Reflects a person's willingness to listen and learn. In our team, humility means recognizing that we don't have all the answers and being open to others' perspectives. It's about valuing every team member's input, regardless of their role or experience level. By fostering an environment where listening is prioritized, we create space for collaboration and collective growth. Humility allows us to stay grounded, continuously improve, and build strong, respectful relationships with our clients and each other.

Strategic

Reveals itself when a creative focuses on the purpose of the goal. At Vers, being strategic means having a clear vision and aligning our actions with our long-term objectives. It's about thoughtful planning, making informed decisions, and leveraging our resources effectively. A strategic mindset enables us to see the bigger picture and navigate complex challenges with intentionality.

Brave

Brave means not being afraid to push the boundaries. It takes courage to be committed to innovation and progress. At Vers, bravery means taking calculated risks and stepping out of our comfort zones in order to challenge the status quo. It's about pursuing bold ideas and standing firm in our convictions, even when we're uncertain. Being brave allows us to explore new frontiers, drive meaningful change, and create impactful solutions. It inspires us to be innovators in our field and constantly push the boundaries of what we can achieve.

Three felt like the right number. Enough to have substance, but still clear and to the point. We sometimes work with clients who have 10 or more core values, and I always find myself wondering what the point is. At that rate, there is no clear lens for leaders to gauge a team's work or culture, and the values will become diluted and forgotten. By focusing on just three core values, we ensured that each one was meaningful and actionable. I wanted humble, strategic, and brave burned into every brain at Vers. Everything we do, and every decision we make, funnel through these key principles.

Deciding on guiding principles is one thing, but implementing them into the life and vocabulary of your team is another. This took time at Vers, but we eventually arrived at a place where our three core values have become a natural part of our daily interactions and decision-making processes. We use them as a metric when we share our "wins" about each other at the end of the week, noting how specific team members' successes happened because they were humble, strategic, or brave. This practice not only reinforces our values but also creates a culture of recognition and appreciation, where everyone is celebrated for their contributions.

Nothing gets me more excited than hearing someone from our team justify a decision they made by referencing one of our values. It shows that our core principles are not just abstract concepts but practical tools that guide our actions. When a team member explains their approach by saying, "I chose this path because it was the most humble and collaborative way forward," or, "This strategy was the most effective for achieving our goals," or, "I took this risk because being brave is part of who we are," it confirms that our values are deeply ingrained in our culture. This alignment ensures that we all move in the same direction, united by a shared commitment to humility, strategic thinking, and bravery. Through this consistent application of our core values, we continue to build a strong, cohesive, and purpose-driven team.

What It All Means

Guiding principles are the backbone of any company. They're not just corporate jargon—they define our identity, purpose, and mission. For every leader, having clear guiding principles is crucial to get the most out of creative teams. These principles create the right boundaries for innovation and creativity and allow teams to experiment while staying aligned with the company's values. As you grow, guiding principles help scale smoothly and maintain your core culture and values. By establishing and truly living by these principles, you'll align the entire organization, boost morale and productivity, and drive long-term success.

When your team understands and believes in a shared mission, it enhances their motivation. This clarity helps them make better decisions on their own, reducing the need for constant oversight. This not only empowers your team but also leads to higher-quality work and a more vibrant, dynamic workplace. Making sure these principles are clear and ingrained in your company's culture is one of the best investments you can make in your team's success and your company's future.

_____
_____
_____

Action Steps

01
Ensure your company's vision and mission statements are clear, concise, and reflective of your long-term goals.

02
Involve key stakeholders through workshops or brainstorming sessions to gather input on guiding principles.

03
Determine and use the core values already evident in your company's culture as a starting point for your principles.

04
Create a set of clear, actionable guiding principles, and refine them based on feedback from trusted stakeholders..

05
Communicate the finalized principles to the entire organization and integrate them into daily operations and decision-making processes.

CHAPTER

Chapter 08

Lie: You can't measure creativity.

Truth: You can always measure the objective side of creative work.

08

The Creative Squeeze

Creativity is a different beast when it comes to business metrics. Unlike something straightforward like measuring the cleanliness of a building, where you have a checklist and clear standards, assessing creative output isn't that simple. Creativity has layers of complex problem-solving, innovation, and subjective judgment that make it tough to pin down with traditional metrics. But here's the thing: even though creativity is hard to quantify, it's crucial that we try. Why? Because in the world of business, what gets measured gets managed. And in creative work, that's just as important as in any other area. When we measure creativity, we're not just looking for a number or a score; we're trying to capture the impact of all those brilliant ideas, those countless hours of brainstorming, and the unique solutions our teams come up with.

The challenge lies in building a framework that respects the nuances of creative work while still giving us tangible insights. It's about finding that balance, recognizing that while you can't measure every brushstroke or brainstorm, you can track the overall impact of the work. So, yes, measuring creativity is complex. It's not as straightforward as ticking off a checklist. But it's essential because when we do it right, we're not just managing creativity—we're empowering it, elevating it, and making sure it drives real value for our organizations.

Chapter 08

When Tensions Arise

Picture this: you're leading a fundraising campaign aimed at generating monthly recurring revenue from Gen Z. Now, as a leader who did not come up with the idea the team landed on, you might not connect with the big campaign idea because, well, you're not the target audience. It's natural to feel that disconnect, but here's where the real challenge—and opportunity—lies.

As leaders, we're wired to make quick judgments. We've built our careers on gut instincts, and those instincts have served us well. But when it comes to creative work, especially something aimed at a different demographic, relying solely on our personal reactions can be a trap. Dismissing an idea because it doesn't immediately resonate with us is a mistake that can stifle innovation and demoralize the team.

This is where data comes into play. Data acts as the bridge between subjective reactions and objective decisions. It allows us to step back from our initial impressions and see the idea through the lens of those it's actually intended to reach. When we're dealing with a campaign aimed at Gen Z, for instance, the metrics, trends, and feedback from that specific audience are what matter—not whether the concept clicks with us personally.

I'm confident I've been the cause of making many creative team members hit a wall when their ideas are dismissed without a fair chance to gather and present this data. They've got the vision, the creativity, and the passion, but without the opportunity to back their ideas with evidence, those sparks of innovation get snuffed out prematurely. It's not just frustrating—it's downright disheartening. I've had countless conversations with talented creatives who feel stuck, not because their ideas lack merit but because they're not given the runway to prove their concepts.

As leaders, it's our job to pull that potential out of them, to create an environment where data is part of the conversation from the start. We need to teach our teams how to validate their ideas with data and how to connect their creative instincts with measurable outcomes. When we do that, we're not just fostering better campaigns—we're empowering our teams to think strategically, to innovate with confidence, and to see their ideas come to life in ways that resonate with the intended audience.

PRINCIPLES PROVIDE THE RIGHT BOUNDARIES FOR CREATIVITY TO THRIVE

Chapter 08

GUT CHECK

Do you believe in measuring creativity?

How do you measure creativity within your organization?

Think about a time you quickly dismissed an idea. Was that decision based on objective data or your gut instinct?
Are you giving your team the space and

resources to validate their ideas with data?

Use Data to Drive Decisions

Logic is your friend when it comes to creative work. The truth is that creativity needs a strong foundation, and data acts as that support. It shapes creative ideas, transforming them from abstract concepts into strategic decisions that drive real, measurable impact. When you equip your creatives with data, you're not stifling their intuition; you're sharpening it. You're giving them the tools they need to take their gut feelings and turn them into evidence-backed strategies. This is crucial because, as much as we might like to rely on our creative instincts alone, they can't always account for the complex, ever-changing landscape of consumer behavior, market trends, and organizational goals. Data bridges that gap, providing a clear reference point that aligns the creative output with the broader objectives of the business.

But here's a warning: don't measure things just to say you measured them. For years, I've sat in boardrooms and worked with executive teams that report on everything from budgets to success metrics—anything but top-line revenues or key mission-driven numbers. The problem is that most of these other metrics can be easily manipulated to look good or bad, depending on the conversation. This isn't necessarily done with ill intent. It's human nature to want to put our best foot forward. However, this tendency can lead to confusion and an incomplete understanding of the real situation.

In board meetings, people don't want to look dumb, so they don't ask questions. If someone reports that the budget looks good, others might not challenge it, even if they have doubts. But it's important to question the most valuable metrics to measure based on what we're trying to achieve. We have to eliminate anything that clouds our ability to get clear results. Think about annual trends. You can track month-to-month data, which can be misleading if you don't consider the broader context. A monthly fluctuation might seem alarming, but it could be irrelevant if that same month shows similar trends every year. It's like a toy company expecting a sales dip in January—Q4 might account for 50% of its annual sales, so a January

Chapter 08

slump is expected. If you're not looking at year-over-year metrics, you're setting people up to fail by focusing on numbers that don't truly reflect the mission's success. You have to measure and celebrate the data that actually matters to achieving your goals.

To really harness the power of data in creative work, you've got to start by establishing a central point of value. This is your North Star—a clear, measurable goal that every project aims to achieve. This value doesn't always have to be a dollar figure, though it will inevitably relate back to one because resources like time and money are finite, and they set the scope of what's possible. Think of it as setting a target—whether it's boosting engagement on a social media campaign, driving conversions on a website, or increasing brand awareness through a new ad. These goals become the benchmarks against which you'll measure your success. Without them, you're just shooting in the dark.

Once you have those goals in place, the next step is to gather data that's relevant to those objectives. This is where tools like analytics platforms, A/B testing, and customer feedback come into play. If your goal is to increase engagement, look at metrics like click-through rates, time spent on the page, or social shares. These numbers will give you insights into what content is grabbing attention and what's being ignored. But remember, data isn't just about looking at what happened; it's about understanding why it happened. This is the human side of data. It's easy to get lost in the numbers, but data should never replace creative intuition; it should complement it. The best creative teams know how to balance the two, using data to inform their decisions without letting it dictate every move.

Data can tell you what works, but it's up to your team to figure out why it works and how to build on that success. Data should foster collaboration, not competition, within your team. Share the insights openly, discuss them, and use them as a springboard for new ideas. When everyone has access to the same information, it levels the playing field, allowing each team member to contribute more strategically. This collaborative approach turns data into a tool for continuous improvement, helping your team grow stronger and more innovative with every project. It elevates your team from being just contributors to becoming essential partners in driving organizational success. Your team will start to understand how their creativity ties into the bigger picture, making them key players in high-level decision-making. When creativity is measured, it's not just about ticking boxes or justifying budgets; it's about turning that creativity into a powerful, strategic force that propels the entire organization forward.

> **DON'T GET LOST IN THE NUMBERS. DATA SHOULD NEVER REPLACE CREATIVE INTUITION; IT SHOULD COMPLEMENT IT**

Chapter 08

Harness the Power of AI

It would be foolish to move forward without acknowledging the power that AI offers when it comes to measuring success. In our rapidly changing landscape, we have to be able to adapt and grow with the technology at our fingertips. That's where AI comes in, bringing a level of clarity and precision that's been hard to achieve until now.

AI can process and analyze massive amounts of data with speed and accuracy that humans simply can't match. This capability allows us to spot patterns and trends we might otherwise miss, giving us deeper insights into what's resonating and what's not. Imagine you're running a multi-channel marketing campaign—AI can sift through engagement data, track user behavior across platforms, and pinpoint exactly which elements of your creative work are driving results. It's like having a data detective on your team, cutting through the noise and delivering actionable insights.

But AI's real value goes beyond just crunching numbers; it actually enhances the creative process itself. With AI, we can shift from reactive creativity when we have to fix things after they've gone wrong to proactive creativity, where we anticipate challenges before they arise. AI can simulate different creative scenarios, letting you test ideas in a virtual environment to see which ones will likely hit the mark. This kind of foresight can save time and money and relieve a lot of headaches.

The Creative Squeeze

AI also allows for a more personalized approach to creativity. By analyzing data on individual preferences and behaviors, AI helps you tailor your creative output to resonate more deeply with specific audiences. In a world where one-size-fits-all solutions rarely work, AI lets you create multiple versions of a campaign, each optimized for different audience segments. This level of customization not only boosts engagement but also builds stronger connections with your target market.

Creative projects often involve a lot of trial and error, which can be both time-consuming and costly. AI streamlines this process by offering real-time feedback on creative iterations. For example, AI can analyze a draft of a video ad and suggest adjustments based on past performance data—whether that means tweaking the color scheme for better visual appeal or refining the messaging to align more closely with audience sentiment. This enables your team to edit faster and with more confidence, knowing their decisions are backed by solid data.

When I think of the key benefits of AI for my team, I see two things. First, I recognize how it enhances collaboration. AI-powered tools can centralize all your data, making it accessible to everyone involved. This transparency fosters a more collaborative environment where team members can easily share insights and build on each other's ideas. AI helps bridge the gap between creative teams and other departments, like marketing or finance, by translating creative metrics into terms everyone can understand. This means that everyone is aligned and working toward the same goals. Second, and in my opinion, the most valuable reason to leverage AI in measuring creative work is that it frees up your team to focus on what they do best: being creative. By automating the more tedious aspects of measurement and analysis, AI gives your team more time to brainstorm, experiment, and innovate. It's not about replacing human creativity with algorithms; it's about enhancing it, and making it more efficient and impactful.

What It All Means

For creative teams, measuring their work isn't just about proving their value—it's about elevating their craft. When creatives track the impact of their ideas with data, they gain clarity on what resonates and what doesn't, allowing them to refine their approach and drive better results. This process transforms creativity from a purely instinctual endeavor into a strategic asset, aligning the team's efforts with broader business goals. Measuring creative work means empowering your team to innovate with purpose, continuously improve, and ultimately contribute to the organization's success in a meaningful, measurable way.

Action Steps

01
Define and communicate specific, measurable goals for each creative project to align team efforts with broader business objectives.

02
Implement tools for gathering and utilizing data throughout the creative process to validate ideas and refine strategies.

03
Train your team to use data patterns and trends to inform and enhance their creative decisions.

04
Adopt AI tools to analyze data, track trends, and simulate creative scenarios for faster, more confident iterations.

05
Share data and insights openly within the team to foster collaboration and ensure alignment across departments.

Chapter 08

CREATIVE

CREATIVE SQUEEZE

One more thing...

The whole point of this book is that you need to put your team first. I've shared lessons I've learned throughout my career—principles that have shaped not only my leadership but also the dynamics of my team. But as I completed the eight chapters, I had a few lingering thoughts.

The Role of Fun in Creativity

What makes someone creative? When I asked my team, they gave answers like curiosity, experimenting with the norm, breaking patterns, thinking outside the box, bravery, tenacity, risk-taking, and having a drive to be different. These traits are awesome and perfectly describe many on my team. But I often wonder if there is some type of molecular makeup that allows some people to be more creative. To me, the simple answer is 'yes.' There are definitely character traits some people have that naturally make them more creative. But there is an action you can recreate even if you're not naturally creative, and surprisingly, it was something the team didn't mention at all. I can guarantee it's something you do all the time without even thinking about it. I might be crazy and have a unique perspective here, but I truly believe the action we can take to become more creative is simply having fun.

I spent my life as the class clown, never taking myself too seriously. This has always been a natural advantage, especially when it comes to creative work and problem-solving, because fun is a necessary part of creativity. But what's interesting is that I have spent a long time writing this book, describing this concept in different ways but never actually cracking the code until now. Creativity often comes from a state of fun, where the pressure of the outcome no longer clouds the thought process. What's the first rule of any problem-solving exercise? "There are no bad ideas," right? But what we don't realize is that the psychology behind that is so simple yet powerful - removing fear is crucial to effective brainstorming. When you and your team can suggest ideas that make you laugh, you break down the barriers of fear, judgment, and the pressure of potential failure, allowing creativity to flow freely. This aspect is often overlooked because it doesn't provide the same immediate satisfaction as crossing a task off a list. We tend to attach our sense of accomplishment to completed tasks—finish the project, give yourself a pat on the back, good job—but true creativity thrives when we focus less on the outcome and more on the process.

> **CREATIVITY OFTEN COMES FROM FUN. WHERE THE PRESSURE OF THE OUTCOME NO LONGER CLOUDS THE THOUGHT PROCESS**

As a leader, it's important to consider how you can build more opportunities for fun into your team's routine.

I promise you that having fun will actually make your creative team better at their jobs. I understand that the idea might seem risky, as if I'm just saying, "let your team have fun," but this isn't something to skip or to cut from the creative process. At Vers, we learned this the hard way. We went through a season where our focus was entirely on completing tasks and maximizing billable hours. While the work got done, we missed out on key opportunities to have fun, and as a result, our creativity suffered. So, we made a change. We started incorporating more fun into our creative processes, like our 10-15 minute icebreakers at the beginning of every staff meeting. This wasn't by accident; it was a strategic move to relax, laugh, and enhance our creative output.

GUT CHECK

I want you to stop here and think back to the most fun environments you've been in over the last 5-10 years. What made those moments memorable?

How did they make you feel?

Are those emotions you want to bring into the workplace?

When I asked my team these 'gut check' questions, one thing stood out: almost every fun environment they described took them back to childhood. Playing board games, screaming on roller coasters, hanging out with friends, and going to the arcade all made them feel like kids again. There was no pressure in these environments. It was just simple. See, the fears that drive our day-to-day go away when we find ourselves in those childlike states. You don't need a high IQ to be more creative; you just need the ability to break down barriers and embrace fun. My point is, don't take yourself too seriously. You and your team will be better off.

As leaders, we must remember that while traits like tenacity, drive, and confidence are essential for success, they don't automatically lead to creative solutions. The real answer lies in fostering an environment where fun and creativity can thrive between people who genuinely trust each other. All of this takes time. Building a successful business is rarely fast, and it isn't cheap. It takes a clear vision and a commitment to your overarching values and mission. But the struggle is worth it. And the things that take a long time to build ultimately take a long time to tear down. All of that leads me to the most valuable lesson of this entire book. It's a value we lean on at Vers and one that should not be forgotten when working towards building a successful creative team - hang onto your allies.

The Role of Allies in Creativity

In the deepest sense, an ally is someone who would take a bullet for you. I know this might sound extreme, but an ally is more than just a person you trust or someone who offers surface-level support. It's beyond being a cheerleader or having your back. Being a true ally is sacrificial—it can hurt. An ally feels the pain alongside you and stands by you through thick and thin. What does this have to do with leading a healthy creative team? Everything.

GUT CHECK

Do you think of your creative team as true allies?

What is something you can do every single day to evaluate and appreciate your allies?

How do you make sure not to take them for granted?

The Work We Do is Impossible Alone

At Vers, our job is to solve the most complex branding and marketing problems for our clients. Often, these challenges require multiple perspectives to be seen from all angles. In Japanese culture, a collective approach to problem-solving is the norm, but in Western culture, we like to romanticize the lone creative genius. The reality is that those are outliers. Some of the best problem-solving comes from a group of minds working together at the same intensity on one problem.

YOUR TEAM MUST BE BOLD IN THEIR EXPERTISE BUT HUMBLE ENOUGH TO RELY ON EACH OTHER

Within your organization, think of your creative teams as your special ops. The work we do is so varied and technically demanding that it's almost impossible for one person to master it all. Our teams come from multidisciplinary backgrounds, bringing expertise in creative theory, strategy, cloud-based development, sales systems, storytelling, writing, design, film, marketing, advertising, customer experience, product development, behavioral psychology, and more. To consistently create remarkable outcomes, each team member must be both brave in their lane of expertise and humble enough to lean on one another.

The Work is More Enjoyable Together

Personally, I find the work more enjoyable when done with people I love and trust rather than doing it alone. There is something to be said about the power of taking a teammate's advice, celebrating the wins together, and leaning on each other when the work gets tough (as it often does). All of that makes celebrating breakthroughs and successes much more enjoyable. There's an incredible satisfaction that comes from seeing the words a copywriter on your team wrote come alive through the voice of a narrator on a short film or witnessing the excitement on a client's face when the results exceed their expectations. If the road to solving any complex problem is tough, you might as well travel it with people you enjoy.

Allies Push

Working with allies brings out the best in everyone. Why? Because allies are the best people to push us. Think about who you turn to when you have a problem. If you're wise, it's the people you trust who will shoot you straight and be honest with you. It's the allies in your life who want what's best for you, even if that means pushing you to do better, to make tough decisions, and to step out of your comfort zone. And you know an ally won't leave you on your own with a problem. They have your back and are willing to stand with you when times get tough.

I have worked hard to create a culture of allies at Vers. I see our team take bullets for each other all the time in various ways. We resist the urge to work in our own silos and truly share the highs and lows of the creative process together. And when you know someone is willing to take a bullet for you, it pushes you to dig deeper and reach your full potential. That's the true power of having allies. The work you do is important, but it might be forgotten in a year, a month, or even a week. Building those relationships, however, is what lasts. As the leader, I encourage you to put your people first. When you do that, you will squeeze the most out of your creative team and achieve lasting success.

Bibliography

University of Oxford. "Happy Workers Are 13% More Productive." University of Oxford News, 24 Oct. 2019, www.ox.ac.uk.

Isaacson, W. (2011). Steve Jobs. Simon & Schuster.

Vance, A. (2015). Elon Musk: Tesla, SpaceX, and the Quest for a Fantastic Future. Ecco.

Henry, T. (2018). Herding Tigers: Be the Leader That Creative People Need. Penguin.

ABOUT THE AUTHOR

Justin Price is a dynamic leader with a proven track record of building high-performing teams, driving organizational growth, and delivering strategic insights at the executive level. Justin's professional journey is driven by his deep-seated passion for helping others push the boundaries of what they believe is possible. In 2014, Justin founded Vers, a full-service marketing agency dedicated to helping nonprofit and cause-based organizations reach their full potential. Under his leadership, Vers has grown into a thriving business known for its award-winning creatives and results-driven strategies. Today, Justin and his team at Vers continue to help organizations reimagine their audience engagement, creating powerful and lasting impacts across multiple industries. With his keen strategic insight and commitment to visionary leadership, Justin remains at the forefront of the marketing and technology landscape, inspiring others to achieve their full potential.

As the author of The Creative Squeeze, Justin shares his wealth of knowledge on cultivating creativity and leading teams toward new horizons of success. His leadership is not just about achieving goals—it's about setting new standards and inspiring future leaders to think bigger, reach further, and transform the world around them.